*Police, Power, and
the Production of
Racial Boundaries*

CRITICAL ISSUES IN CRIME AND SOCIETY

Raymond J. Michalowski, Series Editor

Critical Issues in Crime and Society is oriented toward critical analysis of contemporary problems in crime and justice. The series is open to a broad range of topics including specific types of crime, wrongful behavior by economically or politically powerful actors, controversies over justice system practices, and issues related to the intersection of identity, crime, and justice. It is committed to offering thoughtful works that will be accessible to scholars and professional criminologists, general readers, and students.

For a list of titles in the series, see the last page of the book.

Police, Power, and the Production of Racial Boundaries

ANA MUÑIZ

RUTGERS UNIVERSITY PRESS
New Brunswick, New Jersey, and London

Library of Congress Cataloging-in-Publication Data

Muñiz, Ana, 1984

Police, power, and the production of racial boundaries / Ana Muñiz.

pages cm.—(Critical issues in crime and society)

Includes bibliographical references and index.

ISBN 978–0-8135–6976–5 (hardcover : alk. paper)—ISBN
978–0-8135–6975–8 (pbk. : alk. paper)—ISBN 978–0-8135–6977–2 (e-book
(web pdf) : alk. paper)—ISBN 978–0-8135–7359–5 (e-book (epub) : alk. paper)

1. Discrimination in law enforcement—California—Los Angeles. 2. Community policing—California—Los Angeles. 3. Gangs—California—Los Angeles. 4.
Discrimination in criminal justice—California—Los Angeles. I. Title.

HV8148.L55M86 2015

363.2089'00979494—dc23

2014041066

A British Cataloging-in-Publication record for this book is available from the
British Library.

Visit our website: http://rutgerspress.rutgers.edu

Manufactured in the United States of America

For Alberto

Contents

ACKNOWLEDGMENTS

FIRST, THANK YOU TO the three people without whom this book would not have happened: Kim, Stefan, and Luis. I owe you everything.

Thank you, SoCal/LA Family: The Youth Justice Coalition. To all the LOBOS, Adam, Kruti, Whitney, Diana, Bita, and Hamid: I love you relentlessly. Chris and Xuan, you have all my admiration and respect.

Thank you, Tucson Family: Dad, for teaching me love of justice. Mom, for always giving me a home. Bill, for your unconditional acceptance and support. Beth, for your huge heart. Kate, Alisha, and Soraya, for your brilliance. Wade, Joe, and Dell for the emotional and financial support that gave me peace of mind to focus on writing when things temporarily fell through.

Thank you, Adam and Christina at the Soros Justice Fellowships for your continued belief, concern, and support.

Thank you to the following journals for publishing articles that would morph into chapters of this book: A version of Chapter 3 was previously published as "Maintaining Racial Boundaries: Criminalization, Neighborhood Context, and the Origins of Gang Injunctions" in *Social Problems* 61 (2), 01 May 2014. A version of Chapter 4 was previously published as "Disorderly community partners and broken windows policing" in *Ethnography* (2012) 13 (3): 330-351.

*Police, Power, and
the Production of
Racial Boundaries*

CHAPTER 1

Race and Place in Cadillac-Corning

I AM STANDING IN the back of a dark room. A projection covers the wall in front of me. White letters flicker, "Start a New Simulation." Next to the projection is a beige desk. On the desk stands nothing but a computer. Behind the computer there is a cop. He is white, middle-aged, with brown hair and a bald spot starting in the middle of his head.

A burly white officer with a crew cut stands in the middle of the room, facing the projection. He holds a laser gun. It is hooked up to an oxygen tank that will simulate the reaction of a real gun when it is fired. The officer at the desk says that he will choose a simulation and control it from the computer. The screen flashes the Los Angeles Police Department (LAPD) logo for a few seconds.

Then the sound of automatic fire and a woman's scream. "I've got shots fired!" the officer with the laser gun says. On the simulated projection, a white woman stumbles out from around a corner with blood on her torso. "He shot me!" she screams while tumbling to the concrete. A brown-skinned young man in jeans, a white tank top, and a blue hoodie appears from around the corner. "Drop the gun!" the laser gun officer commands. The hoodie-clad young man walks briskly toward the camera with a gun in his right hand. "Back the fuck up!" the young man on the projection shouts, then stops. He points the cold black gun at his right temple. The LAPD officer fires the laser gun once into the young man's head as he simultaneously blows his own virtual brains out. The screen freezes. The officer exhales, slams his gun in his holster. "Nice!" the officer manning the computer laughs from his office chair.

The officer who shot the simulated man in the head turns and says, "Now we are going to do a debrief." He explains that the Force Option Simulator is "really used for articulation. We find that officers are shooting at the right time and they are hitting what they shoot at. But when investigators come in, officers are not articulating what they saw. Why they pulled the trigger." He continues, "A debrief like this helps officers to articulate what happened." The officer at the desk cuts in, "Investigators focus on three things: tactics before, during and after; when you unholster your gun; and when you re-holster your gun."

The officer at the desk asks the laser gun officer why he drew his gun. The officer who did the simulation responds that he realized it was a dangerous situation. He took his gun out and got in position. As the suspect raised the gun toward the laser gun officer, "I shot in defense of my life." He puts his hand to his own chest as he says this in a show of sincerity. "And I decided to shoot him one more time after he put a bullet through his own head." He laughs a little, then quickly catches himself and switches back to serious mode, "I saw the gun moving forward. But look at the background. Even though I would have been justified in shooting, it probably wasn't the best decision because . . ." He points to the screen. A red circle shows where the officer's gunshot landed. The bloody woman from the beginning of the simulation is lying in the background. One red circle hovers right in front of her head.

The officer holds out the laser gun to me, "Now it's your turn." How on earth did I get here?

I am reminded of *Waiting for the Barbarians*, which is the title of both an early 20th-century poem and a late 20th-century novel (Cavafy 1972; Coetzee 1980). Both pieces of work are stunning. Both tell the story of a society's preparation for an invading barbarian army that never arrives. In the novel, an unfamiliar official of the Empire enters a village. He has been dispatched from the capital to prepare frontier towns for an inevitable war between the Empire and the barbarians. The official claims that the barbarians are arming themselves and uniting their forces to reclaim land from the Empire. He has no evidence. In fact, people of the Empire rarely encounter the nomadic barbarian tribes. Nonetheless, he is sure there is reason to fear an invasion. People traveling the trade routes have been attacked. Who else could it be but the barbarians? Officials sense they are being trailed, watched from a distance. Who else could be responsible but a coordinated army of barbarians? The narrator of the novel remains skeptical of the barbarian invasion:

Once in every generation, without fail, there is an episode of hysteria about the barbarians. There is no woman living along the frontier who has not dreamed of a dark barbarian hand coming from under the bed to grip her ankle, no man who has not frightened himself with visions of barbarians carousing in his home, breaking the plates, setting fire to the curtains, raping his daughters. Show me a barbarian army and I will believe. (Coetzee 1980, 9)

Panic over the idea of a barbarian army eventually undermines the physical and social structures of the town. The soldiers set brush fires to burn the barbarians out of hiding. But no barbarians come scurrying from under the smoke. The fires destabilize the land. Embankments of weakened soil collapse, flooding part of the town. Barbarians are blamed. The soldiers take what they like from the local stores and do not pay. They rob houses. The economy is in shambles. A good chunk of the citizenry has fled. The town is underpopulated, barren. For the remaining people in the village, "There is nothing to do but keep our swords bright, watch and wait" (Coetzee 1980, 44). When stories of the feared barbarians stop, people assume it must be because the soldiers are too busy fighting off the barbarians to send news.

Every so often, the army of the Empire goes on a journey to capture a dozen or so "barbarians." The soldiery parades the captives, wrists bound, into the town square. The townspeople gather. Officers announce that these chained nomads represent a large, fierce army. They must be publicly tortured. The townspeople joyfully participate in the whipping so relentlessly that the soldiers have trouble maintaining order.

Like the officers of the Empire in Coetzee's book, authorities in Los Angeles, alongside neighborhood watches, neighborhood councils, and other community groups, conduct a frenzied search for a tattooed homeboy. Every once in a while the police conduct a high-profile raid. They parade people of color in front of cameras, hands bound behind their backs, heads down, shirts off. The people they call "barbarians" look like my family and friends. But I guess for other people they are threatening foreigners to be waited for with sharpened swords. Alleged "gang members" are the shadowy specters in modern-day Los Angeles.

The allegory here is pretty clear. Inside and outside of the field of criminology, the construction of and moral panic over the dark, dangerous criminal (i.e., the barbarian) has been commented on extensively (Glass-ner 1999; Harcourt 2001; Sampson and Raudenbush 2004; Davis 2006; Hinkle and Weisburd 2008). There is a lot of figurative waiting, scapegoat-ing, suspension of rights, and pre-emptive attacking of so-called barbarians.

I want to take a step back. Panic happens after a barbarian has been identified. But how are the visions of barbarians created in the first place? I am here, in this room, being handed a laser-tag gun because I want to see the process of creation. As the narrator in Coetzee's (1980, 145–146) novel says to an officer in the Empire's army, "I am only trying to under-stand. I am trying to understand the zone in which you live."

The term "gang member" has become natural, accepted. Lawmakers use the term to justify punitive policies. When a black or Latino man is shot, there is a good chance police will claim he is a gang member. News outlets will uncritically repeat the report with a headline like "Gang Member Shot in South LA." The *Los Angeles Times* reports that people are gang members so often that they explicitly clarify when they are talk-ing about people of color who are not alleged to be gang members. For example, on November 25, 2013, a young black man was shot to death in rush-hour traffic. The *Los Angeles Times* article on the murder stated that the victim "was not involved with gangs" (Santa Cruz 2014). Portions of the general public grasp the gang-member construct with fear, hatred, and racist ideology. A small portion of that public has the power to act on the fear, the hatred, and the racist ideology. They are why I am here.

I am in no way saying that violence is not real. The shootings between neighborhoods that occur too frequently are not social constructions. My argument is that the violence committed by the state (police and city prosecutors, in particular) is both ethically reprehensible and ineffective at ending street violence. Repressive policies exacerbate violence on the street by locking people into a life of constant state surveillance, harass-ment, brutality, and detention that restricts their opportunities to lead stable lives. Locking up large numbers of people or trapping them inside their homes will probably reduce crime—for a little while. But that is not living. Bringing the hammer down in one area may push the problem to another area. But that is not real public safety. This book is my attempt to understand, with my community, how people in power continue to implement repressive policies and how we can intervene to create true, sustainable safety for all neighborhoods.

MAY 2012: HOW MANY COPS DOES IT TAKE
TO WRITE TWO TICKETS FOR SOME WEED?

The correct answer is nine. At least it is in the Cadillac-Corning neighborhood of Los Angeles. Four cars—the entire patrol for the West Los Angeles Police Department Division—are blocking my back gate. The Los Angeles air is turning cool as the smog tints the sunset fuchsia. Two white male officers are speaking with two young Latino men. A Latino male officer oversees another two young Latino men who are cuffed with legs uncomfortably spread and faces silently pointed toward a maroon wooden fence. One of them is a neighbor from down the street. That leaves six officers standing around, talking, smiling with one another, casually leaning against patrol cars enjoying the show, taking an occasional break to shoot me a bad look. I do not want to piss the cops off more. They will take it out on these youth by detaining them when they otherwise would not have or by subjecting them to rougher treatment. I also know that I can look deceptively respectable on the right day and might be able to intervene. Since I am returning from court in a nice dress and heels, today is one of those days. I walk near them and ask the officer what is happening. He tells me to back up. I ask my neighbor if he needs help. He turns his shaved head slightly in my direction. "Could you go tell my mom? She's inside. Thanks." An officer grabs me by the arm. "Ma'am, do not converse with the suspects!"

I go to the neighbor's house to find the mother of one of "the suspects." I have glittering memories of that house—celebrating birthdays, dancing, and eating too much pollo asado. When I return, the officers are dispersing, two by two in their patrol cars. First, one car slowly backs down the alley. Then another drives out the opposite direction. A bald-headed white cop and his partner get in their car and floor it, speeding backward down the alley. Another car follows. Nine officers responded to the call. The result: two Chicano youth with tickets for possession of small amounts of marijuana.

What happened to elicit the response just described? This book examines how police, city prosecutors, wealthy residents, and business owners identify and exclude supposedly dangerous people from the Cadillac-Corning region of Los Angeles. How do these people collaborate and clash in attempts to direct police resources? What beliefs, knowledge, data, and frameworks are central to how they act upon what they perceive to be danger? I explore these questions focusing on community partnerships between residents and the police. When I use the term "community partnerships" I refer to programs that bring the police, organized residents, and, at times, other relevant government agencies together to develop problem-solving projects as fear reduction and crime prevention strategies. In community partnerships, law enforcement and residents struggle to reinforce racial and class boundaries through competing ideas about policing and social control. In particular, I explore the tension that exists in trying to meld broken windows policing and community policing in Cadillac-Corning, a Los Angeles neighborhood that has been a flashpoint for repression-oriented policing since the 1970s.

Community policing involves cooperation between police and residents in the development of crime prevention strategies. Broken windows policing (also called "order-maintenance" or "zero-tolerance policing"), however, places emphasis on order maintenance by officers with community members in a supporting role. Proponents of the broken windows theory argue that the accumulation of small acts of disorder (litter, graffiti, the presence of truants, loiterers, people who are homeless, and street vendors) creates an environment conducive to serious crimes like robbery or assault. Preventative policing grants the police discretion to target signs of disorder to prevent escalation to violent crime (Wilson and Kelling 1982; Bratton and Malinowski 2008). Because Los Angeles acts as a model for other cities in both law-enforcement tactics and organizing against police abuse, this topic has national relevance, particularly in the current era of zero-tolerance policing.

In trying to make sense of the police response illustrated in the opening anecdote, I am concerned with what occurred behind the scenes in the days and weeks prior as well as in the years and decades before. I look at important historical junctures in order to understand how the current hyperpolicing of Cadillac-Corning came to be. A key theme here is how the Cadillac-Corning region of Los Angeles became a predominantly working-class African American enclave that, by the 1960s, was viewed by people outside the area as a neighborhood with a violent reputation. Changes in housing development and school desegregation were central to the formation of the neighborhood. The demographic changes set the stage for repressive policing. The creation and implementation of Los

Angeles City's first gang injunction solidified Cadillac-Corning's stigmatization in the 1980s.

A gang injunction is a restraining order, not against an individual, but rather against an entire neighborhood. If subject to an injunction, alleged gang members are not allowed to engage in behavior that is otherwise legal, including congregating in groups of two or more and standing in public for more than five minutes. Since the injunction, Cadillac-Corning has been a test site for repressive policies and practices that eventually spread to the rest of the city.

I do not describe the dynamics of control, force, and power in Cadillac-Corning simply for the sake of building theory. Bridging theory and practice does not happen by producing more theory. Instead, youth organizers and I used the research to challenge the use of gang injunctions in California. Overall, this book mixes a scholarly analysis of domination with real-world case studies of challenges to that domination.

THE ACADEMIC CIRCUS

I had never lived anywhere but Tucson, Arizona, until I moved to Los Angeles to attend graduate school. I don't think anyone I knew from Tucson had moved away, either. I drove away from my home because something told me that I needed distance in order to understand it. That year, wildfires seared the hills around LA. Though only a state over, when I reached California I felt painfully disconnected from my family and the land itself, my temple of sweeping desert. I had no spiritual connection to the sea. How was I going to wake up without the smell of creosote or fresh tortillas or the sound of thunder? I watched the green of the Border Patrol shift into the blue of the LAPD as dirt transformed into concrete.

In grad school I found white people studying people of color. There were people of color studying people of color. There were people pretending to be homeless. Much urban ethnography is concerned with using "deviant" low-income people of color as research objects to be alternately feared and pitied by highly educated voyeuristic consumers of ethnographic texts (Kelley 1998). One grad student, after she was done at her so-called field site—a street filled with homeless youth—would remove her ragged hoodie and slide a giant diamond back into place on her ring finger. In an ethnographic methods class, she once told a horror story about another researcher witnessing a gang shooting. The girl feared for her life afterward. She just wanted to watch. But now her hands were soiled. I was the only one who did not convey sympathy. My sympathy was with the people directly suffering the violence daily.

"You are angry." I hear this often. Of course I am angry. I am tired of seeing people I love, many of them young people, locked up or murdered. Some of the murders have been because of street violence. Others were executions by police. All were the result of repression-oriented policies and practices that made our neighborhoods unsafe. People stood by and took notes on it, shook their heads, examined computer models of homicides, and said, "How interesting." Yes, this makes me angry. Anger is part of the method.

The opening vignette to this book is one of the only moments in which I will briefly speak about residents who are not part of community groups. The sole reason for including the vignette is to provide context, to illustrate a situation common in Cadillac-Corning. In my research, rather than focusing on what authority considers deviant, I directed my energy upward, studying the entities primarily responsible for subjugation. Instead of donning rags, I played dress up in business attire. Instead of studying gangs, I looked at the process by which the term "gang" became a legitimate, racialized way of ordering the world. I questioned the meaningfulness of the concept by interrogating how police, city prosecutors, wealthy residents, and business owners struggled to conceptualize, identify, and control deviance. During the first part of my research, from the summer of 2007 to the summer of 2010, I lived in the 18-square-block Cadillac-Corning neighborhood.

I did not move into the neighborhood for research purposes. When I visited the University of California, Los Angeles (UCLA), I immediately loathed its community of Westwood and most of the surrounding area. Cadillac-Corning was within commuting distance but sufficiently far removed from West LA culture. And the people there reminded me of home. My research questions did not come from academic literature but from the daily experience of constant patrol cars, stops, sweeps, and choppers. I noticed that police activity changed just outside of the boundaries of Cadillac-Corning. I wanted to understand why.

As a first step, I began attending regular monthly meetings and town halls held by community groups that participated in crime prevention partnerships. The community groups consisted mostly of residents from neighborhoods surrounding Cadillac-Corning and a few homeowners from within Cadillac-Corning. I was struck by how residents, prosecutors, business owners, and police spent entire meetings vehemently complaining about Cadillac-Corning as well as by how they collaborated on repressive strategies. It was also apparent, however, that civilians and law enforcement often conflicted with one another on their assessment of proper tactics in the neighborhood. In fact, the residents were often more militaristic than the police. Community group members were not representative of neighborhood residents. Their high levels of formal community involvement made them unique. It is precisely this uniqueness and unrepresentativeness, however, that interested me. Community groups planned to shape the neighborhood in specific ways. They reached out to leaders in local government, the LAPD, the City Attorney's Office and to business interests to control access to the neighborhood, resource distribution, the appearance of the area, and the behavior of residents.

As I continued to attend meetings, I became acquainted with the community group members. They seemed excited to have a relatively young person attend their meetings. I was in my early twenties at the time, and because of a round face and curly hair, I tend to look younger than my age. They also were happy to have a resident of Cadillac-Corning (there were not many others) and a Latina (there were no others) at the meetings. I became known as the UCLA student who was writing about their efforts.

Community group members who worked closely with the City of Los Angeles introduced me to employees in the LAPD and the Los Angeles City Attorney's Office. Some were willing to give me their time because they liked talking to me or had done projects when they were students in which they interviewed officials. Some had their egos fed by my interest in their work. A couple of men told me I was beautiful, so that probably had something to do with their willingness to meet with me. I accessed the LAPD West Division COMPSTAT (complaint statistics) meetings during the research period, and I accompanied officers and prosecutors on their daily routines. I then entered the archives to look at the history of housing, gang injunctions, and police tactics in Cadillac-Corning.

In 2011 I laid out every piece of data I had collected over the previous three years. I decided I did not want to trademark any new terms.

There were already too many. I was trying to figure out how this riot of words could be made useful to something other than the electronic archive of dissertations.

I have grown to love LA wildly, but I did not at first. I encountered the Youth Justice Coalition (YJC) upon my arrival in Los Angeles in early 2007. Organizers at the YJC work to build a youth, family, and prisoner-led movement to dismantle Los Angeles County's and California's juvenile injustice system. The YJC is one of the nation's few organizing projects led by young people, ages 7 to 24, who have been or are currently under arrest, on probation, in detention, in prison, on parole, or on gang injunctions or whose loved ones have been incarcerated for long periods of their lives and/or deported. The YJC uses direct-action organizing, advocacy, action research, policy development, political education, and activist arts to end the massive lockup and deportation of people of color; widespread police violence, corruption, and distrust between police and communities; the vicious "war on gangs" that tracks and traps youth as young as 10 in gang databases and injunctions; the school-to-jail track that prioritizes zero tolerance, school push-out, and arrest; and the operation of the world's largest network of prisons and jails (www.youth4justice.org).

The pull of the YJC, my West Coast family, held me and fed me until I got my balance. They infused me with the life that was dripping away. I knew my work could be useful at the YJC. I wanted to work to make it useful. From 2011 to 2013, I worked with the Youth Justice Coalition to conduct a community study on gang injunctions and develop a model of community-based, youth-led research. I trained and provided guidance to youth organizers who analyzed statistical data, conducted surveys, used GIS (geographic information systems) to map four injunction neighborhoods, and carried out ethnographic fieldwork. Much of the research in the first four chapters of this book provided the background for the Youth Justice Coalition research, which is presented in Chapter 5.

LIFE IN CADILLAC-CORNING

Cadillac-Corning is a predominantly working-class black and Latino immigrant neighborhood. It sits on the edge of the West Los Angeles police jurisdiction, which includes some of the wealthiest neighborhoods in the country. There is lively foot traffic, particularly in the early morning and late afternoon. Mothers lead their children to and from the nearby elementary school, high school students skateboard between home and class, vendors sell fruit, gardeners load plants and tools in the back of their trucks, neighbors talk to one another across their fences, and people rush to the nearby bus routes. Before school, many students stop at Joe's Market on Cadillac, a tiny convenience store near the elementary school that has been there for over 50 years. The neighborhood consists primarily of two- and three-story apartments built in the 1960s, punctuated occasionally by a single-family home built in the 1920s. Most apartments are surrounded by wrought-iron fences, some with spikes pointing inward, that were installed in the 1970s and 1980s. The housing is dense, with narrow alleyways in between and behind apartment buildings. Parking along both sides of every street essentially creates one-lane roads throughout the neighborhood.

According to the 2010 Census, 86% of all occupied housing in Cadillac-Corning was renter-occupied units. Sixteen percent of residents in Cadillac-Corning were white, 18% were black or African American,

FIGURE 1 Apartment building in Cadillac-Corning with wrought-iron fence, spikes pointing inward. Photo by the author.

FIGURE 2 House on the northern border of Cadillac-Corning: A sudden transition from apartments close to the street to a seemingly suburban space of single-family homes with spacious lawns. Photo by the author.

and 59% were Hispanic or Latino (U.S. Bureau of the Census 2010a, 2010b). At the time of this writing, income information for 2010 was not available. The median household income for the 2000 Census, however, was $28,180. Thirty-two percent of families lived below the poverty level (U.S. Bureau of the Census 2000b).

Crossing the street to a surrounding neighborhood is an abrupt change from dense city life to an almost suburban space of trim lawns, ample parking, quiet sidewalks, and large houses. For example, in 2010, 66% of residents in the census tract to the north were white, 9.5% were black or African American, 8.5% were Asian, and 11% were Hispanic or Latino (U.S. Bureau of the Census 2010c). In the 2000 Census, the median household income was $45,641 with only 9% of families below poverty level (U.S. Bureau of the Census 2000d). The area to the north included more owner-occupied units and more whites than Cadillac-Corning. Furthermore, according to the 2000 Census, the inhabitants

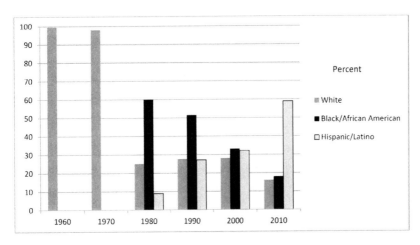

FIGURE 3 Race in Cadillac-Corning, 1960 to 2010. Source: U.S. Bureau of the Census (1960a, 1970, 1980a, 1990a, 1990b, 2000a, 2010a, 2010b).

in the renter-occupied units to the north had higher incomes than those in the Cadillac-Corning census tract.

The tract to the immediate west, which includes Beverlywood Estates, had a drastically different composition than Cadillac-Corning, with 93% of all occupied housing owner-occupied (U.S. Bureau of the Census 2010d). The area to the west was 86% white, 1.5% black or African American, 5.5% Asian, and 4% Hispanic or Latino (U.S. Bureau of the Census 2010d). In 2000, this area had a median household income of $114,097, with only 2% of families below poverty level (U.S. Bureau of the Census 2000e, 2000f). Chapter 3 provides extended data on race and socioeconomic status in Cadillac-Corning from 1960 to 1980. Many of the residents in the surrounding neighborhoods are upper-class, white, and Jewish.

For nearly four decades, the police, the City Attorney's Office, organized business owners, and homeowners associations in bordering neighborhoods have tried to alter Cadillac-Corning in various ways. The neighborhood served as a site of experimentation in which policies and protocols were developed before they were spread to the rest of the city, state, and country. For example, in 1987 the gang injunction that would serve as a model for all ensuing injunctions was first implemented in

Cadillac-Corning. In 1997, Cadillac-Corning was a site for the SARA (Scanning, Analysis, Response, and Assessment) model. The SARA model is a problem-solving policing method in which officers collaborate with neighborhood prosecutors, landlords, and community groups to fight crime, blight, and quality-of-life offenses. The SARA method is now widely used by police departments nationally. Today in Cadillac-Corning, local groups of wealthy, politically expedient residents and business owners strategize about how to direct police and prosecutorial efforts.

The analysis here provides rare, firsthand qualitative work outside of New York City on the newest policing craze—broken windows. In 2003, former New York City Police Commissioner William Bratton brought the broken windows philosophy to Los Angeles with missionary zeal. The broken windows theory is now gaining popularity among police departments nationally. In Cadillac-Corning, police struggle to define disorder, neighborhood boundaries, and community among elite citizens who have the power to challenge them.

Youth Justice Coalition organizer Kim McGill (personal communication) argues that the nation's most repressive policies against youth originated in LA: "If you can starve this beast, then you can transform the world." Now, let's try to first understand the beast.

CHAPTER 2

A Neighborhood Is Born

HOUSING DEVELOPMENT, RACIAL CHANGE, AND BOUNDARY BUILDING

IN 2003, A BLUE sign went up at the intersection of Cadillac Avenue and La Cienega Boulevard. The sign boasted the city seal of Los Angeles and the name "La Cienega Heights." A dozen or so people in a community group voted to rename the neighborhood. They were hoping the new name would "rehabilitate" the neighborhood's status. But the new veneer has not buried a reputation decades in the making. There are still whispers about Cadillac-Corning at homeowners association meetings in the surrounding wealthier, whiter neighborhoods. A thirty-something white man with dark-rimmed glasses confided to a fellow Beverlywood Homeowners Association member, "I drive Cadillac every day. My wife is terrified." A young pantsuit-clad woman gasped in response, "Oh my god, I would be scared too."

The concept of "neighborhood" seems simple. People use the term all the time to describe collections of blocks. But how do these spaces come to be understood as neighborhoods in the first place? How does there come to be a general understanding that one area has an identity that is distinct from another across the street? Before delving into the stigmatization and policing of Cadillac-Corning, I am going to tell the story of how Cadillac-Corning came to be an African American and Latino neighborhood surrounded by more affluent white and Jewish inhabitants, thus, setting the stage for militarization and suppression.

The ideal of the single-family home was central to Los Angeles's sprawling development (Fishman 1987, 156–157). Los Angeles was the land where everyone could have a car and where everyone's backyard was assaulted by year-round sunshine. The first houses were built in the

Cadillac-Corning area in the 1920s. Through the 1930s and 1940s, architect and Bel-Air developer Elwain Steinkamp built Spanish-style houses and duplexes characterized by tile roofs, courtyards, and large glass windows (Oliver 1989). The shopping center where a Ross Dress for Less discount store and CVS drug store now stand was a dairy farm at the time. Bill, a Jewish man who lives just south of Cadillac-Corning, grew up in the area and graduated from Hamilton High School in 1966. He recalled, "Most of the time I was there it was about 90 percent white and about 80 percent Jewish."

Laura, a black female Cadillac-Corning resident, graduated from Hamilton in 1971, when desegregation was in full swing. She was born and raised in an adjacent middle-class neighborhood. She moved in after attending college in 1977 when her parents helped her find an apartment. They thought the area was safe, affordable, and close enough that her sister, a student at Hamilton, could visit after school. Laura remembered, "My parents were ok with me living in an apartment because of the house and apartment mix. There were not just apartments on the street." Laura explained that when she first moved in, many apartment buildings were owned by individuals, "So they were very mindful of the type of tenants they rented to. The type of tenant they rented to was a lot different than what's available now. When the big management companies started to purchase the buildings and take them over, there just seemed to be a shift in the type of person that you would see living in the neighborhood." Building permit documents and city council case files confirm Brenda's observations that new apartments were built by individual owners living on the property or within several blocks. Between 1960 and 1965, many of the neighborhood's current apartments were originally built.

THE FIGHT FOR PREUSS ROAD: "TENEMENTIZATION" OR NEEDED DEVELOPMENT?

Preuss Road sits on the western border of Cadillac-Corning. The case files from a requested zone change provide insight into the lives of some homeowners in the area as well as the state of housing in the area during the 1960s. The conflict over the proposed rezoning ordinance demonstrates that the actions of individual homeowners can reshape the neighborhood physically and socially, with effects that last for decades afterward.

Sam Ladin, the owner of two properties on South Preuss Road applied to the City Council to have the zone changed from R2-1 (duplexes) to R3-1 (multiple units) and the building setback line changed from 25 to 15 feet. The building setback line determines how close to the street a building can extend. The request for a smaller setback line indicates plans to construct larger buildings on the property. He unsuccessfully attempted the changes in 1955 and again in 1963. Residents opposing the zone change cited five primary reasons for their resistance: It would ruin the residential character of the street, cause overcrowding, strain local services, and reduce property values, and there did not exist demand for new development in the neighborhood.

In the 1963 case, a married couple on Preuss Road wrote in a letter,

I purchased the property and moved into the area because of the existing deed restrictions limiting the area to private residences. A change in zoning would destroy the residential character of the neighborhood and deprive my family of the benefits of our property. . . . Also there is no need for additional units in this area. The adjoining streets to the East, Shenandoah, Bedford, Sherbourne, etc., are already zoned for multiple units, yet many single family dwellings still remain and very many of the apartment buildings have "for rent" signs. . . . Finally, a 15' setback eliminates lawns and planting areas, creates a tenement-like neighborhood, and completely destroys the character and value of the residential homes remaining. (Levenson and Levenson 1963)

The reasons stated by these homeowners were repeated in other letters of opposition. Several residents stated that they bought their homes because the of deed restrictions that guaranteed a residential area. Couples and families placed import on living among "nice, quiet" single-family residences (Stevenson and Stevenson 1963). In addition to changes in lifestyle that the zone change would bring, residents also worried about lowered property values. Opponents claimed that Preuss was still a high class residential area with "2-story residences in the $40,000 to $60,000 class" on the edge of a neighborhood being "tenementized" ("Building Setback Line" 1963, 1; also see Baum and Baum 1963). They believed that apartment development "would only overburden the school, the fire protection facilities, and the police departments in the area" and "result in the parking of many more automobiles and our already crowded streets" (Stevenson and Stevenson 1963).

Opponents of the ordinance reveal what the state of development was in the rest of the area by 1963. A report by opposing residents claimed that current apartments were not filled, indicating a lack of need for further development.

According to the document "Building Setback Line" (1963, 1),

> A survey of the area immediately east of Preuss Road extending to La Cienega Boulevard discloses that in this area, which has already been zoned R3-1, there are 138 lots currently containing one-family bungalows and 19 containing duplexes or 4-flat buildings, all of which are susceptible to development as multiple dwellings under the existing zoning in the area, in addition to which in this same area, there are 64 multiple dwellings, 36 of which show existing vacancies.

The city planning commission report confirmed the change from single residences to multiple dwellings:

> There are eleven (11) multiple dwellings in the 1900 block of Preuss Road at the present. The block to the south is 69% multiple dwellings; the block to the east is 71% multiple dwellings. . . . The area has undergone a complete change from single residences and R2-1 to multiple dwellings in the past eight years. Construction is still going on. (Roberts and Davis 1963)

It appears that the boundaries of the neighborhood were implicitly set by 1963. Officials and residents referred to the area between La Cienega Boulevard and Robertson Boulevard as a unit to be internally compared. By 1963 most of the streets in the neighborhood were already zoned for multiple-unit apartment buildings. Preuss represented an anomaly.

1920s	First houses built in Cadillac-Corning area
1955	Homeowner zone change attempt on Preuss fails
1961–1966	Interstate 10 Freeway construction
1963	Homeowner zone change attempt on Preuss fails

Several residents also wrote letters of support. Some Preuss Road residents wanted the opportunity to supplement their income by building additional housing. For example, one woman wrote,

> When Mr. Sam Ladin first filed a request for change of Zone from R2-1 to R3-1 1900 Block Preuss Road, Tract 1250 several years ago my late husband and I definitely disapproved and worked against it. . . . Now that we are completely surrounded by apartments and as there are now seven or eight courts in the 1900 block of Preuss Road why should we not be allowed the same privilege of building income apartments on our property as others have in this area. We have large lots adequate for such income buildings. We are also paying exorbitant taxes for the privilege of keeping our homes. (Harton 1963)

Several residents cited prohibitive taxes as the motivation to build multiple units on their property (Minear 1963):

> We are writing as property owner [*sic*] at the above address. My husband and I have lived here for twenty-two years. We have enjoyed the area of single family dwellings until the passed [*sic*] few years and now multiple units are being built around us.
>
> As pensioners, the only [way] we can continue to live in this neighborhood is to build an apartment house and live in one of the units.
>
> The rise in surrounding property values has been reflected in a higher tax rate for our old home. We will be able to build an apartment house because we have the cooperation of our family.
>
> The zone change to an R-4 will make it possible for us to pay a higher tax with this improvement. As things are now, we have a hard time paying our taxes without any additional income.

Dissatisfaction with taxes could indicate the early stirrings of the 1970s tax revolt. In 1978 California passed Proposition 13, a state constitutional amendment that decreased property taxes and restricted annual increases (O'Sullivan, Sexton, and Sheffrin 1995). Although property taxes did not rise sharply until 1973, some scholars trace inordinate tax burdens for homeowners and the seeds of revolt to the mid-1960s (Sears and Citrin 1982).

Also, some homeowners viewed the eventual development of Preuss as inevitable:"This is not a high class residential area. We are surrounded by apartment houses and courts. In fact the 1900 block on Preuss Road is the only 1900 block from La Cienega Blvd. to Robertson Blvd. which still remains R2-1" (Tlacil 1963).

The rezoning request was rejected on the basis of resident opposition and insufficient demonstration of demand for additional housing in the area. However, the request was successful when Stanley Bernson, the owner of a lot on Preuss Road, applied for it seven years later in 1970. Although the City Planning Commission suggested that the ordinance not be adopted, the City Council overrode their opposition. At the hearing for the proposed zone change, 17 residents appeared in favor, 12 in protest.

As opposed to their rejection of the request in 1963, the City Council justified their approval in 1970 on the basis of increased demand for housing:

> There has been a significant change in circumstances since the previous disapproval of R3 zoning in 1963. Since 24 (41 percent) of the 58 building sites within a 300 foot radius have changed from single or duplex type buildings to apartments in the last five and one-half years, this shows a significant trend in the development of the area during said period.
>
> Those in favor of the zone change including the applicant's representative stated that the circumstances have changed in the area since the last request in 1963. Besides, a very low vacancy factor for apartments, the existing zoning is C-2 on the west and R-3 on the east and south. They are of the opinion that the present R-2 zoning has become inappropriate and unrealistic in the view of the old dwellings and changing character of the neighborhood. ("Motion" 1970)

By 1970, the neighborhood was nearly equally split between single-family homes and multiple-unit lots. The city council report states that east of Preuss Road to La Cienega Boulevard there were 250 lots with single-family homes and 207 parcels containing apartments, duplexes, or four-flat buildings ("Motion" 1970).

The city council report also states that during the 1963 request, Interstate 10 was in process of being constructed, during which a large amount of property zoned for multiple units was demolished (City of Los Angeles Department of City Planning 1969, 9). Interstate 10 passes a few blocks south of Cadillac Avenue. From 1961 to 1966 the city demolished swaths of apartment housing on the edge of Cadillac-Corning to clear a path for the new freeway.

The action of a homeowner on Preuss changed the possibilities for property owners on the whole street. The homeowner who petitioned to have the zone changed also confirmed the changes that were already happening on streets around Preuss. Officially rezoning the street formalized a phenomenon in progress—the development of homes into apartments. Similar rezoning and apartment development occurred in a domino effect on streets throughout the area in the 1960s, the amalgamation of which created a series of blocks that were distinct from others nearby. This distinct unit of blocks came to be known by residents, law enforcement, and government agencies as a neighborhood.

1966	Exclusive Apartments, Inc., zone change attempt on Chariton successful
1970	Homeowner zone change attempt on Preuss successful

The Arrival of Property Management Companies

While most of the development included one to five additional units on a property, some property owners demolished homes and built large complexes. For example, in 1960 a man who lived on Guthrie Avenue built a two-story, 22-unit apartment complex on property the next block over. The complex also included a 21-car garage and a swimming pool (City of Los Angeles Department of Building and Safety 1960). The next year, 1961, another homeowner on Guthrie developed a three-story, 14-unit apartment building on Corning Street (City of Los Angeles Department of Building and Safety 1961a).

A few people who lived outside the area bought and developed property in Cadillac-Corning during the 1960s development boom. On Chariton Street, homes were demolished to make way for two 15-unit apartment complexes (City of Los Angeles Department of Building and Safety 1961b, 1962). Small companies began to purchase and develop property in the 1960s as well. In 1966, Exclusive Apartments, Inc., successfully changed the setback line to 15 feet on five lots on the northeast side of Chariton Street. The change brought the five lots in line with rest of Chariton, which already had a 15 foot setback line. Exclusive Apartments, Inc., demolished the homes on the lots and constructed apartment buildings (City of Los Angeles Department of City Planning 1966, 4).

Landlords with large apartment complexes increasingly sold their property to management companies. The trend accelerated during the 1970s and 1980s. This is the second wave of housing changes that determined the composition of Cadillac-Corning. The entrance of large property management companies is significant for two reasons. First, several management companies combined properties to construct larger complexes. Instead of one to three units, apartments swelled sometimes to 20 units or more. Second, property managers lived off site. The link between renters and tenants was looser, perhaps allowing for more egalitarian rental practices. Property management companies began accepting Section 8 renters (people entitled to governmental low-income housing assistance). Rental prices decreased, and tenants stayed for shorter periods of time than they had previously. Lower-income renters with a shorter tenure may have been to whom Brenda, the longtime resident quoted in the beginning of this chapter, was referring when she said, "When the big management companies started to purchase the buildings and take them over, there just seemed to be a shift in the type of person that you would see living in the neighborhood." The changes in housing were followed by the demographic change from a Jewish to African American residential area, a shift that was important in the development of Cadillac-Corning's reputation.

INTEGRATING HAMI HIGH: "WHEN THE SCHOOL GOES ALL BLACK, THEN THE NEIGHBORHOOD GOES ALL BLACK"

During World War II, employment in the defense industry brought large numbers of African Americans to Los Angeles. The rapid expansion of the aerospace industry and the establishment of military bases opened up new job opportunities. Until 1948, racially restrictive covenants to maintain "neighborhood stability" were common throughout the United States

(Collins 2006; Gordon 2008, 71). African Americans were confined to the southern part of the city.

After the war, Jews also migrated to Los Angeles in large numbers. Jewish veterans from across the nation purchased homes in Los Angeles. Despite being shut out of the WASP (white Anglo-Saxon Protestant) downtown elite by a wave of anti-Semitism in the 1920s, Jews were able to enter retail, Hollywood, and Westside real estate. Consequently, Jewish elites formed a Westside power center around Century City, just west of Cadillac-Corning (Leonard 2003).

Hamilton High School ("Hami High") opened in 1931. In the mid 1960s, Hamilton and the surrounding neighborhoods were still overwhelmingly white, Jewish, and upper middle class. The Los Angeles Unified School District (LAUSD) adopted an open-school transfer policy for integration purposes in 1954 (Turpin 1967b). The open-school transfer policy in theory allowed students to enroll in schools outside of their neighborhoods if space was available. It was not until the mid 1960s, however, that the LA School Board actually issued open-transfer permits to minority students. As we will see later, transfer permits were used to send black youth to predominantly white schools, to kick black youth out of white schools, and to help white youth flee predominantly black schools. The Unified School District experimented with methods to encourage racial integration.

For example, in January 1967 the LA Board of Education commenced the Mid-City Secondary Education Project, slated to last at least one year, to encourage voluntary integration. Seven-hundred and fifty students were voluntarily bused to 10 specialized instruction centers, one of which was Hamilton High School (Turpin 1967a). As black parents transferred their children west from predominantly black schools, they found Cadillac-Corning was one of the few affordable places on the Westside.

1931	Hamilton High opens
1954	LAUSD adopts open-school transfer policy
1966	LA School Board issues open-transfer permits to minority students
1967	Mid-City Secondary Education Project begins voluntary integration

FIGURE 4 September 20, 1963: Members of the Congress of Racial Equality, local clergy, and Hamilton High School students hold a hunger strike at a Los Angeles Board of Education meeting to protest segregation. John Malmin Copyright 1963. *Los Angeles Times*. Reprinted with permission.

Hamilton was central to integration struggles on the Westside of Los Angeles. Jewish and black groups formed (sometime uneasy) coalitions to end school, housing, and employment segregation, white supremacist violence, and police brutality (Eley and Casstevens 1968; Lockard 1968; Greenberg 2006). In the wake of World War II, the Holocaust, and the Red Scare, black and Jewish organizations allied to challenge institutional anti-Semitism and antiblack racism (Collins 2006, 27). For example, when Proposition 14 passed in 1964, repealing the 1963 Rumford Fair Housing Act, only Jewish and black communities voted overwhelmingly against the proposition (Leonard 2003, 48). The Rumford Fair Housing Act prohibited discrimination by property owners and landlords on the basis of ethnicity, religion, sex, marital status, physical handicap, or familial status.

On Friday, September 20, 1963, members of the Congress of Racial Equality, local clergy, and black and white students from Hamilton and other high schools began a hunger strike at a Los Angeles Board of Education meeting to protest a special report on de facto segregation. Many of the white students cited their Jewish background as motivation to participate in the protest. A 17-year-old female Hamilton student remarked, "I went to temple first. Then I thought I would do something more for my religion and my country" (*Los Angeles Times* 1963).

The Board of Education also fielded demands from predominantly black South Los Angeles high schools, like Jordan, and East Los Angeles high schools, such as Roosevelt and Garfield (McCurdy 1968). East Los Angeles high schools pushed for bilingual instruction, more Mexican American administrators, quality food, improved building conditions, and a ban on corporal punishment. Students were transferred to other high schools as a disciplinary measure for their participation in civil rights protests. Several black students who attended Hamilton on transfer permits had their permits canceled for political activity, sending them back to their schools of origin (*Los Angeles Times* 1973d).

Increasing numbers of white parents sought transfers out of Hamilton, especially to the nearly all white Culver City High School. In 1968, 8% of Hamilton students were black (Faris 1970). By 1970, the number of black students reached 20% in a student body of 3,000 students. The same year, Hamilton's white enrollment dropped 22% from the previous year (*Los Angeles Times* 1973d). By the 1971–1972 school year, black enrollment had reached 34%, and minority enrollment was at 43%. In 1972 black-white enrollment reached a 50-50 split (Smith 1972). For the first time in district history, the Los Angeles Board of Education banned transfers of minority students into and white students out of Hamilton in order to "racially stabilize" the school (Greenwood 1972). Only two other schools were included in the ban, middle schools that were also on the Westside.

1963	Hunger strike at the LA Board of Education
1965	Watts uprising
1970	Hamilton qualifies as an "inner-city school"; the California Supreme Court finds the LA School Board guilty of intentional segregation
1972	The LA Board of Education bans transfers permits at Hamilton

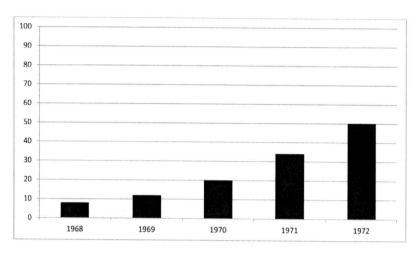

FIGURE 5 Percentage of black students at Hamilton High School. Source: Faris (1970); Smith (1972); *Los Angeles Times* (1973d).

School board policies were implemented in the area of the city where the maintenance of segregation was most under threat. Transfers were banned in the borderland spaces where the affluent Westside bumped up against the corridor to the south and east of the city. School segregation and housing segregation relied upon one another because housing prices were (and are) tied to the quality of public schooling (Haurin and Brasington 1996; Figlio and Lucas 2004; Kane, Staiger, and Riegg 2005). The transformation from a white to a black Hamilton facilitated a parallel change in Cadillac-Corning, and vice versa.

The white migration from Hamilton was later reflected in Cadillac-Corning. As one white parent moving from the area warned, "When the school goes all black, then the neighborhood goes all black" (*Los Angeles Times* 1973d). By 1973, only 40 of approximately 800 black students at the school were bused. Most black students lived in the neighborhoods surrounding the school.

Throughout the city, upwardly mobile Jewish families moved to more affluent neighborhoods (Leonard 2003). White Jews with light skin color and job skills were able to move into entrepreneurship and white-collar work by the 1950s. However, they retained a presence as landlords to new Cadillac-Corning residents. According to Neil C. Sandberg,

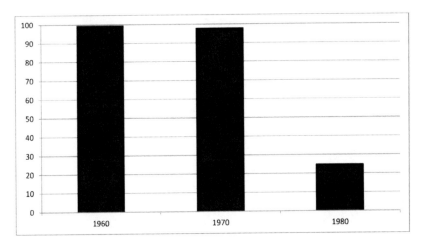

FIGURE 6 Percentage of whites in Cadillac-Corning. Source: U.S. Bureau of the Census (1960a, 1970, 1980a).

American Jewish Committee regional director, many Jews concerned about Black Nationalism and anti-Semitism had pulled away from solidarity with blacks. Hoping to prevent further Jewish flight, the American Jewish Committee held meetings to engage residents on the racial change in neighborhoods and schools (Jones 1970).

In 1960, Cadillac-Corning was 99.6% white (U.S. Bureau of the Census 1960a). Most of the residents were professional, managerial, clerical, or sales workers (U.S. Bureau of the Census 1960b). Twenty-three percent of the population was foreign born, mostly from Poland and Russia (U.S. Bureau of the Census 1960c, 1960d). The surrounding areas were similar in their racial and class makeup. In 1970, Cadillac-Corning was still about 98% white (U.S. Bureau of the Census 1970).

The 1980 Census tells a completely different story. Over the course of the 1970s, Cadillac-Corning had become 25% white, 60% black, and 9% "Persons of Spanish Origin" (U.S. Bureau of the Census 1980a). The census tract to the north was 72% white (U.S. Bureau of the Census 1980b). The area to the west, which includes Beverlywood Estates, was over 90% white (U.S. Bureau of the Census 1980c). The average household income (in 1979 dollars) in Cadillac-Corning was $15,802 (U.S. Bureau of the Census 1980d). To the west, it was over $50,000, and 97% of housing units were owner occupied (U.S. Bureau of the Census 1980e, 1980f). The areas surrounding Cadillac-Corning remained the predominantly white, Jewish, and upper middle class, while Cadillac-Corning became an increasingly working class, African American island.

GOODBYE GOLDEN AGE: RACE, MILITARIZATION, AND THE MEDIA

In 1973, the *Los Angeles Times* issued a five-part special on Hamilton. The series portrayed Hamilton so negatively that white transfers surged after it was printed, and the *Los Angeles Times* then issued a statement highlighting Hamilton's positive attributes and encouraging white parents to keep their kids at the school (Zuckerman and Bleviss 1973). Principal Josephine Jimenez complained several years later that the reputation of the school never recovered from the series of articles (Curtis 1984). The first article was entitled "Boredom and Tension Replace 'Golden Age.'" The special grieved for the downfall of a segregated Hamilton:

> Once it was the very image of an All-American high school on the suburban fringes of Los Angeles. Now it is an urban high school, with all the pressures and troubles which accompany that change in status. Apartment houses and homes surround the rear and two sides of the 21-acre campus, while the Santa Monica Freeway and a somewhat weary commercial district of small stores and businesses are its close neighbors to the front.
>
> Some veteran members of the faculty look yearningly back on that period and call it Hamilton's golden age. Their memory is of classrooms full of parent-prodded, anxious-to-succeed students who did not question a teacher's authority and who often bit off more work than they were even assigned. It was, says one teacher, "like an exclusive prep school" (*Los Angeles Times* 1973a).

After the Golden Age, white teachers, students, and administration accused black students of bringing violence, drugs, conflict, and militancy to school. At one point, when a fire damaged the first floor at Hamilton, white parents and teachers initially blamed black students for imitating the 1967 Detroit and 1965 Watts uprisings, which were sparked by police actions in black neighborhoods. It was later discovered that a white student started the fire (Faris 1970).

The *Los Angeles Times* articles detailed white students' fears:

Whites talk in apprehensive tones about being jostled in the halls or not using the bathrooms because they might be beaten up or exhorted for loose change by blacks. . . .White students tend to shun school dances and athletic events at night, largely because they or their parents fear violence at the hands of blacks. . . .There are white students who stay away from school dances because blacks laugh at the way they dance. One coach, lamenting the problems he has getting some white boys to go out for sports, thinks the youngsters are not only unsure they can measure up to blacks athletically, but are also fearful of them. (*Los Angeles Times* 1973d)

Teachers struggled with educating a racially and socioeconomically diverse classroom. One Hamilton teacher commented, "It's not unusual to have a kid who is the son of a doctor and another who is from a family of seven and does not know who his father is in the same class" (*Los Angeles Times* 1973c). Teachers complained that students were less willing to take commands than in the old days, and they exhibited more "attitude." For the first time in district history, the teachers union went on strike to demand a greater role in administrative decisions.

In 1970, Hamilton qualified for the first time as an "inner-city school." The new designation earned Hamilton resources for 13 additional teaching positions. Some of the positions were converted to hire armed security agents instead of educators (*Los Angeles Times* 1973b). Hamilton administrators started to lock the school's gates during school hours, and LAPD cars regularly patrolled the perimeter. As black students entered Hamilton in greater numbers, the school became more militarized. Suspensions and arrests of black students rose steeply. Black students complained that they felt as if they were in a prison. A *Los Angeles Times* staff writer recounted the school's daily disciplinary routine: "The signal that a security agent is needed is one bell, sounded throughout the school by a control device in the school's main office. One hears it periodically during the day, and it is a somewhat ominous sound. Everyone knows there is a problem, and maybe trouble." One armed security agent bragged, "We don't slap them on the hand, put it that way. If they're definitely wrong, they'll be booked" (*Los Angeles Times* 1973e).

In 1978, LAUSD announced that no student could transfer to a school in which the student's racial group already made up more than

50% of enrollment (Trombley 1980). Hamilton's humanities and music magnet programs were started to encourage voluntary integration—this time of white students. In 1979, the Board of Education planned to move the magnet school from Hamilton's campus to a site in Temescal Canyon, a white and wealthy community off the Pacific Coast Highway and Sunset Boulevard. If whites could not stop black students from moving into the school, maybe they could move the entire school. Their attempt to move the school was halted by a judicial review that warned of hardship on minority students and opposition from homeowners and environmental groups (Trombley 1979; Baird 1980). The judicial review reminded the board's lawyer of the 1970 California Superior Court decision that found the board guilty of intentional segregation in the location of new schools and setting of attendance boundaries.

By 1984, minorities made up 78% of the student population. Instead of moving their kids away, some white parents tried to lure whites back and reverse Hamilton's "brain drain" (Curtis 1984). Parents in the affluent Cheviot Hills and Beverlywood neighborhoods held public meetings to convince their neighbors of the desirability of Hamilton, stressing its safety and academic performance. When that was unsuccessful, luring turned to pulling. Parents threatened to sue the school district unless they investigated the number of students who had illegally migrated out of Hamilton to schools more west and more white. Parents replied that they would just enroll their children in private school rather than return to Hamilton.

| 1981 | Hamilton humanities program started |
| 1994 | Proposition 187 passed |

CONCLUSION: BUILDING AND REINFORCING NEIGHBORHOOD BOUNDARIES

By the early to mid-1960s the current boundaries of Cadillac-Corning emerged. Although it had not been named, residents in the area, members of the City Council and City Planning Commission, and reporters referred to the blocks between Robertson Boulevard, La Cienega Boulevard, Sawyer Street, and Cadillac Avenue as a neighborhood. City institutions played a large part in establishing the boundaries of Cadillac-Corning.

The 1960s constituted a shift in the physical and social landscape of the area that would eventually become known as the Cadillac-Corning neighborhood. Cadillac-Corning became a site for multiple-unit housing development on the Westside through the efforts of middle-class home-owners. Residents fought on both sides of the struggle for multiple-unit development, sometimes for surprising reasons. City government, how-ever, was the gatekeeper of change. Permission to develop new hous-ing relied on the approval of city planners. The administrative bound-aries laid out in planning reports and ordinances overlaid the informal neighborhood boundaries already known by locals. The second wave of housing development occurred when management companies purchased properties and built large apartment complexes. The clusters of apart-ments solidified the neighborhood boundaries. Hamilton High School was another catalyst for the racial and class changes that occurred in the surrounding area. People looked to the high school for indicators of racial change, socioeconomic status, and safety in Cadillac-Corning. The school and the neighborhood makeup were mutually reinforcing.

Cadillac-Corning has a legacy of hosting marginalized groups. Ini-tially, Jews moved west into the area to gain access to employment and housing. Forty years later, black families migrated west into Cadillac-Corning for the same reason. Currently, Cadillac-Corning is home to recent Latino immigrants in search of the same things—reasonably priced housing, proximity to employment, and quality education for their chil-dren. For generations, the neighborhood offered opportunities to groups rejected elsewhere in the city, acting as a narrow passageway into the affluent Westside.

What do changes in zoning, housing development, and school deseg-regation have to do with gang injunctions, broken windows, and commu-nity policing? In order to develop and implement repressive policies, law enforcement needs a geographical target area to criminalize. They need to be able to distinguish the target area as exceptional and threatening to justify such policy changes. During the time of contested school desegre-gation and white panic over rioting, researchers were hard at work trying to devise ways to manage what they called "black disorder" and "mob behavior." Up until the Watts uprising in 1965, riots had been the result of white mobs, backed by police, blowing through black and brown neighborhoods, beating and killing residents, destroying businesses, and burning homes. With Watts, black residents armed themselves and fought back, to the surprise and terror of white civilians and government officials. Up north in Palo Alto, Stanford psychologist Philip Zimbardo was conducting experiments in which he planted an abandoned car in public to observe the conditions under which it would be vandalized (Harcourt 2001, 131–132). James Q. Wilson and George L. Kelling (1982) later used the study as the centerpiece of their broken windows theory, named for the window Zimbardo had to shatter with a sledgehammer to incite "respectable whites" to collective vandalism of the car. In the broken windows theory, however, the bodies of disorder would be brown and black, not respectably white. The inherit racism of broken windows informs gang injunctions and community policing.

From the 1960s onward, Cadillac-Corning became categorized as a high-density, lower-income, predominantly black area. Multiple-unit housing development and school desegregation were central to the race politics that enabled recategorization. The exceptionality of the neighborhood made it a lightning rod for repressive policing tactics. The ecology of the neighborhood made it an intermediate space in which defense of racial boundaries could be enacted. Because Cadillac-Corning represents a passageway to the Westside, some try their hardest to close it off. The first three Los Angeles Board of Education school transfer bans occurred at schools in the same area of the city. The gang injunction was another method by which police and city prosecutors fought to maintain race and class boundaries. Through the injunction, authorities also cemented the stigmatization of the neighborhood and were even responsible for the name Cadillac-Corning.

CHAPTER 3

Maintaining Racial Boundaries

CRIMINALIZATION, NEIGHBORHOOD CONTEXT, AND THE ORIGINS OF GANG INJUNCTIONS

HOUSING DEVELOPMENT, SCHOOL INTEGRATION, and racial change in the 1950s through the 1970s distinguished Cadillac-Corning from surrounding areas. Consequently, Cadillac-Corning was an easy target for containment and control tactics in defense of bordering white middle-class neighborhoods. By the 1980s, Cadillac-Corning's stage was set as a training ground for the newest policy of repression—the gang injunction.

In the 1980s, Los Angeles street gangs were exploding into popular consciousness. Rock cocaine was about to become big business. During a 1987 court case involving Cadillac-Corning residents, an LAPD officer pleaded with the judge, "Can you imagine meeting 15 year old kids who have $5,000 cash in their back pocket? Or meeting a high school junior who has the keys to a brand new Mercedes?" (*City of Los Angeles v. Playboy Gangster Crips* 1987b). A probation officer in the Cadillac-Corning area reflected the frustration of the police and the city prosecutors with the juvenile system: "Try to rehabilitate some of them if you can. I tried at first to help some of the kids, but I soon learned that it was a wasted effort" (*City of Los Angeles v. Playboy Gangster Crips* 1987c). Law enforcement officials had been locking up black youth in Cadillac-Corning, but they argued it had not worked. Probation had not worked either. They wanted a more powerful tool.

Law enforcement would have their prayers answered in the form of a gang injunction. Injunctions are civil lawsuits against neighborhoods based on the claim that gang behavior is a nuisance to nongang-involved residents. Injunctions then restrict the movements of those labeled gang members. Police officers have the discretion to decide who is served with an injunction (Caldwell 2010). In addition to naming 10–30 specific people on the injunction, prosecutors also list hundreds of John Doe's, to be identified at a later point (Myers 2009). If alleged gang members are listed on an injunction, they are not allowed to engage in behavior that is otherwise legal, including—but not limited to—congregating in groups of two or more, standing in public for more than five minutes, wearing certain clothes, and making certain gestures. They can be arrested if they engage in any of these activities. Alleged gang members can be subject to enhanced sentences of 10 years upon conviction. Gang injunctions are civil orders. Consequently, unless the enjoined are on probation or parole, they are not entitled to public defenders if they choose to appeal the order.

Gang injunctions are most popular in Southern California. As of January 2013, there were 46 gang injunctions targeting over 80 neighborhoods in the City of Los Angeles alone (Office of the City Attorney of Los Angeles 2013). Injunctions can cover the geographic area of one neighborhood block or several square miles. One injunction in Los Angeles County covers 16 square miles (Los Angeles County District Attorney's Office 2011). Alleged gang members may also have their personal information, social contacts, and tattoos entered into the CalGang Database. By 2003, 47% of African American men in Los Angeles County between the ages of 21 and 24 were on the Los Angeles County CalGang Database (Siegel 2003).

The gang injunction model has begun to spread; to date, civil gang injunctions have been obtained in at least seven states beside California (Maxson 2004). Britain has implemented gang injunctions targeting minors (GOV.UK 2013). In addition to spreading to other cities, the injunction has been expanded to target other groups as well. Los Angeles police and city prosecutors have also recently used injunctions to target drug dealing in skid row, attack graffiti crews, and halt Occupy protests. One of Southern California's most recent injunctions was implemented near Disneyland shortly after vehement community protest in response to the murder of unarmed Manuel Diaz by Anaheim police. Thus the gang injunction model is being used to police political behavior as well as "criminal deviance."

The model for the modern-day gang injunction was designed in the Cadillac-Corning neighborhood with the 1987 injunction against the Playboy Gangster Crips (PBGs; Myers 2009, 288). It is perhaps surprising that Los Angeles City's first gang injunction was implemented in Cadillac-Corning. It was not the area with the most murders or assaults. Cadillac-Corning, however, was a threat to the boundaries of white, middle- and upper-class areas. Part of the reason Cadillac-Corning was targeted for the injunction is that it threatened geographic racial and class separation and control. Despite the sanitization of race in gang injunction policy, fear of black men and stereotypes about black families were central to the rationale for the injunction. Race is central in the evidence that was presented to attain the injunction. The injunction was meticulously designed to control the movement of black youth by criminalizing activities and behavior that is unremarkable and legal in other jurisdictions. Thus, the injunction shored up racial boundaries.

To understand the origins of racialization in gang injunctions, it is necessary to understand the neighborhood in which it began. The Cadillac-Corning injunction became an archetype through a high-profile court struggle, a "critical juncture" that set the pattern for future injunctions (Mahoney 2001). Critical junctures occur when an institutional response is created to address a problem. Future actors are likely to use the policy set at the critical juncture (Gains, John, and Stoker 2005; Levin-Waldman 2009). In the 1980s, the Los Angeles Police Department and Los Angeles City Attorney's Office tailored the prohibitions and the practical implementation of the injunction to the neighborhood with close attention to its racial dynamics and physical layout. Law enforcement sought to control the movement of black youth and upset the Playboy Gangster Crips' drug operation through the criminalization of routine behavior in a target area. Attorneys decided what to enjoin through observation of the gang in the context of the neighborhood. Since then, a protocol has been established to produce boilerplate injunctions. The rules are in place, but the politics that produced them have disappeared from view. What remains is the criminalization of racial groups and target spaces under the guise of a routine race-neutral policy.

RACIAL CRIMINALIZATION, GANG INJUNCTIONS, AND NEIGHBORHOOD CONTEXT

Compared to other areas of sociological inquiry, literature on gang injunctions is relatively sparse. Most social science research on gang injunctions assesses their effectiveness in reducing crime rates in hot spots. The results, primarily from quantitative studies, are mixed: Some find slight short-term reductions in crime (Grogger 2002; Maxson, Hennigan, and Sloane 2003; O'Deane 2007); while others conclude that injunctions do not address the root causes or long-term effects of gang violence (ACLU Foundation of Southern California 1997; Klein 1998). Tracey M. Meares and Dan M. Kahan (1998) argue that gang injunctions could reduce visible gang activity through the establishment of new community norms, while enhanced sentences communicate to other youth the legal consequences of gang involvement. Edward L. Allan (2004, 240) views gang injunctions as "far less draconian than other civil remedies used to curb gang activity" because they do not explicitly target the families of alleged gang members. Allan (2004, 240) and others (Livingston 1997) also argue that injunctions avoid arbitrary enforcement by differentiating "hard-core members of targeted gangs" from "innocent" people as well as limiting enforcement to specific locations, people, and conduct.

Alternative literature demonstrates, however, that injunctions displace violence into adjacent areas without addressing the root problems (ACLU Foundation of Southern California 1997; Klein 1998). Moreover, crime rates and calls for service are notoriously inefficient measures of actual crime. The LAPD has been caught underreporting and misclassifying crime reports, possibly to meet crime-reduction targets (Poston and Rubin 2014). Researchers also find that police often fail to include the community in the development process of injunctions (Miranda 2008). In a rare study that includes interviews with people listed on gang injunctions, Beth Caldwell (2010) argues that injunctions may encourage gang activity. Caldwell examines the injunction against the Venice Shoreline Crips in the gentrifying Oakwood area, concluding that gang injunctions increase isolation among alleged gang members and other neighborhood youth. Gang injunctions amplify the multiple levels of marginality already suffered by people in gang injunction areas (Caldwell 2010, 260; also see Vigil 2003; Hennigan and Sloane 2013).

First, Caldwell found that by leading to the incarceration of low-level peripheral members, the injunction tied individuals closer to the gang. People were exposed to networks in prison and jail that they otherwise might not have encountered. Second, putting the label of "gang member" on people encouraged them to adopt the identity, rather than shaming them out of it (Becker 1997). Third, the gang injunction destabilized the entire community by creating tension between residents and law enforcement. Last, the injunction precluded alleged gang members from participating in positive community activities. The injunction inhibited opportunities for family formation and employment—the very activities that help people leave gangs (Caldwell 2010, 262–263).

The myopic focus on crime rates misses the overarching effect gang injunctions have on marginalized communities (Boga 1993; Stewart 1998; Roberts 1999; Barajas 2007; Bickel 2012). In particular, scholars assert that gang injunctions are used to control black and Latino communities through mechanisms of criminalization. First, injunctions criminalize communities of color by stigmatizing public space in target neighborhoods. Mundane behavior by residents in injunction areas becomes defined as deviant. Law enforcement is consequently able to remove alleged gang members from public space, not because they have committed a crime, but rather because they are allegedly gang affiliated and therefore threatening to middle-class elements.

In this sense, injunctions draw heavily from the broken windows theory of policing in which the accumulation of small acts of disorder (litter, graffiti, the presence of truants, loiterers, people who are homeless, and street vendors) supposedly creates an environment conducive to serious crimes like robbery or assault. Preventative policing grants the police discretion to target signs of disorder in order to prevent the escalation to violent crime (Wilson and Kelling 1982; Bratton and Malinowski 2008). Despite official race neutrality in the language of the broken windows theory, the disorderly people targeted by police are overwhelmingly lower-class, black, and Latino and are using public space (Harcourt 2001; Parenti 2001). Alex Alonzo (1999) and Frank Barajas (2007) also note that gang injunction neighborhoods tend to border areas that are undergoing revitalization projects and have increasing property values. Injunctions allow law enforcement to remove low-income youth of color from white, middle-class residential areas and commercial centers.

Second, gang injunctions criminalize not just a select group of alleged gang members but entire racial groups. Gary Stewart (1998) argues that gang injunctions employ a façade of race-neutral language to control the movement of communities of color through the use of gangs as a proxy for low-income urban blacks and Latinos. Stewart compares modern gang injunctions to the Black Codes, vagrancy ordinances that targeted blacks specifically after the Civil War in an attempt by Southern officials to regain control over former slaves. Black Codes, like gang injunctions, labeled a marginalized group as inferior and deviant and created a dual-track criminal justice system: one for protected whites, and another for African Americans that guaranteed their captivity (Bickel 2012).

Like the Black Codes, gang injunctions criminalize a broad range of mundane activities within the target community. Anyone who fits the racial profile of gang member is subject to stops, detainment, and enhanced sentencing. Those who socialize with people already classified as gang members are often categorized as gang associates and subject to police harassment and detainment (Santos and Romo 2007). Through gang-association charges, entire families, groups of friends, and neighborhoods become entangled in gang injunction restrictions or torn apart by prohibitions on socializing.

An understanding of the origins of gang injunctions elucidates the literature on racial threat and neighborhood context. Previous research demonstrates that the percentage of young black men present is positively associated with the perception of high crime in a neighborhood, independent of actual crime rates (Quillian and Pager 2001). Donald P. Green, Dara Z. Strolovitch, and Janelle S. Wong (1998) found that crimes against Asians, Latinos, and blacks in New York City were most prevalent in traditionally white areas that experienced an in-migration of minorities. The power-threat hypothesis predicts that white violence will be highest where there is a nonwhite economic and political challenge to white standing (Blalock 1967; Tolnay, Beck, and Massey 1989). Green, Strolovitch, and Wong (1998), however, found no relationship between racially motivated crimes and economic conditions, such as the rate of unemployment, indicating that violence against minorities was not due to economic competition. Rather, white residents were defending their neighborhood from the simple presence of an increasing nonwhite population. The change in a balance between white and nonwhite residents sparked white defense of territory.

Research also demonstrates that police use greater amounts of force depending on neighborhood context. Officers are more coercive in neighborhoods with higher homicide rates (Terrill and Reisig 2003). Scholars also find a "defended white neighborhood" phenomenon among police. Black youth face the greatest discrimination by police in predominantly white areas that recently experienced an influx of African Americans (Stewart et al. 2009).

The classification of urban low-income black and brown people as alleged gang members is a dominant justification for heavy surveillance, control, detainment, and harsh sentencing in Los Angeles. Like nearly all classification systems, the classification of neighborhoods as target areas and people as gang members is a site of social and political struggle. However, after a classification system has been in place for a while, the messy politics behind the creation of the system are forgotten (Bowker and Star 1999, 45). Successful innovations spread through mimicry (DiMaggio and Powell 1983). Over time, classifications are naturalized or disguised as purely technical, and the entities that created them become invisible (Sennett 1980; Bowker and Star 1999). The act of forgetting includes the removal of authors from bureaucratic documents, the obscuring of the physical sites in which classifications and protocols developed, and erasure of the political negotiations that determined classifications.

Many researchers assess whether or not gang injunctions work (Livingston 1997; Meares and Kahan 1998; Grogger 2002; Maxson, Hennigan, and Sloane 2003; Allan 2004; O'Deane 2007). But to ask that question, to take gangs as the object of analysis, takes for granted the legitimacy of the definition of gang membership in the first place and its racialized way of ordering the world.

To the Corner of
Cadillac and Corning

In the 1980s, John, a white male, was a city prosecutor assigned to the West Los Angeles area. As we sat in his office on a sunny spring morning over 20 years later, he remembered asking West LAPD officers at the time what the worst area in the division was. They took him to the corner of Cadillac Avenue and Corning Street. The neighborhood gained its name from the intersection that was infamous among West LAPD officers. In an interview, an LAPD Officer who worked Cadillac-Corning explained, "It was just the two major streets where all the activity was. It was where all the problems were occurring. Officers knew that's where you go when you want to pick up some crimes."

Cadillac-Corning, however, was far from being the most dangerous area of Los Angeles. When the 18 LAPD divisions are ranked for crime rates, with 1 being the highest crime rate, 18 the lowest, that is, the safest area, West LA was one of the safest places in LA during and before the time of the gang injunction. From 1980 to 1987, the West LA Division had a homicide rate that was 14th or lower for six out of the eight years (ranking 12th in 1981 and 13th in 1982). For the same time period, the West LA Division was 17th or lower in aggravated assaults. For robberies and vehicle thefts, West LA moved up a little in numbers but never reached the top half of divisions with the highest rates. From 1980 to 1987, residential burglaries fluctuated, with West LA ranking, respectively, the 5th highest of the divisions, 11th, 12th, 6th, 8th, 12th, 13th, and 15th. There was one area in which West LA consistently had the sixth to ninth highest rates—Part II offenses, which include other assaults, fraud, embezzlement, and so-called quality-of-life offenses such as vandalism, vagrancy, and disorderly conduct (Los Angeles Police Department 1980–1987). The higher prevalence of Part II offenses would be consistent with arguments that the purpose of gang injunctions is to target "undesirables" such as the poor, young, and minorities (Boga 1993; Stewart 1998). However, in none of the categories, especially violent crime, was the West LA area most in need of intervention relative to the rest of the city.

Nonetheless, John learned all of the ins and outs of the Cadillac-Corning neighborhood. In an interview, he explained that he spent a year riding in police cars, covertly filming the PBGs' early morning hour drug operations and talking to residents. He identified what behavior to enjoin on the injunction through his conversations with authorities and residents as well as his own in-depth observations of the neighborhood. He paid close attention to mundane routines, including city services.

The Los Angeles City Attorney's Office and the LAPD compiled a binder that was a crude early version of the current digital gang database, which catalogued people John could identify as PBG members or associ-ates of the gang. When I spoke with him, John remembered, "We were not sure if it was ethical or legal. We had a list in our drawer, and if we got this person arrested, fuck 'em as bad as we can no matter what." The binder was filled with the names and faces of black youth. In his testi-mony, an LAPD officer made apparent who would be targeted in the injunction: "It's funny. If you walked or drove through RD 869 [Cadillac-Corning], you'd think the neighborhood just has young black males by the looks of who dares to walk outside." In court testimony, he character-ized black gangs as far more threatening than Latino gangs:

> They don't even do the things that you'll sometimes see the Mexican gangs do, like play football or have a picnic. They have only one pur-pose in life . . . to profit from crime. . . . Unlike the Mexican gangs where there is a very strict hierarchy and strict decisions as to who will commit a crime, in the black gangs there is less respect for that hierarchy and all the players are scrambling to be the number one guy. (*City of Los Angeles v. Playboy Gangster Crips* 1987d)

The greater comfort with Latinos extended beyond gangs into ste-reotypes about family values, competence, and morality. In an inter-view, John argued that the police initially ignored black gangs based on assumptions about family structure:

> Hispanic gangs came from families with very strong family values. You're not supposed to say it but it was real clear that in the black culture they didn't have that kind of value system that Hispanic fami-lies had. And it carried over into the gangs. . . . A lot of times in the early, in the mid-eighties, the feeling was as bad as it gets, and you could call this maybe prejudice in a way, but the black gangs will never get it together. It was like, yeah, Hispanic gangs sold more pot. Black gangs are more ruthless, at the time they were at least, and sell-ing, you know, and selling crack cocaine but they're not organized. You know, one person will kill another one in a second. And that was true, there was only so much respect for their hierarchy. Law enforcement kind of rested on their laurels thinking they will never get to be really organized because we see in the black community they can't pull their families together.

Early on, authorities saw the PBGs and black gangs generally as a problem. They did not, however, expect black gangs to be able to run an organized drug operation. Regarding the difference between the Italian Mafia, the Brown Shirts of Nazi Germany and black gangs, an officer testified, "All that's is [*sic*] missing is the intelligent gang member who has a head on his shoulders" (*City of Los Angeles v. Playboy Gangster Crips* 1987d). According to law enforcement, black gangs were violent, "ruthless," savagely aggressive, immoral, and out of control (*City of Los Angeles v. Playboy Gangster Crips* 1987d). But they supposedly did not have the smarts that Italian-American gangsters or German Nazis possessed.

Law enforcement quickly realized their mistaken assumption about social disorganization as they tried unsuccessfully to stop the PBG's flourishing drug trade. Individual arrests by undercover officers did not stop the overall operation. In his declaration to the court John stated, "For every gang member caught dealing rock cocaine, there are two more to take his place" (*City of Los Angeles v. Playboy Gangster Crips* 1987e). The court testimonies are further filled with amazement that a black gang had such a "sophisticated communication network," "elaborate escape routes," and "an organization that's run more like a business than you would believe" (*City of Los Angeles v. Playboy Gangster Crips,* quoted respectively at 1987e, 1987a, 1987d). The authorities grudgingly admitted that the alleged gang members were not as stupid and disorganized as they had assumed them to be.

The process behind the production of the injunction reveals not just whom it was crafted to control but also whom it was supposed to protect. Since the 1970s, Cadillac-Corning has been a predominantly working class black (and later Latino) neighborhood surrounded by middle- and upper-class white Jewish areas. A city prosecutor commented in an interview, "We had a community just north of Sawyer. The single-family homes, you know, 18th Street and Airdrome, where you could like, rob people or burglarize their houses to feed the drug dealers, to get your drugs, then you go back and you rob again. . . . It was kind of like a circle because you had pockets of wealth all around this gang, drug user kind of haven."

A police officer at the time said in court, "We also believe they are heavily involved in robberies in the surrounding communities, from

Beverley Hills to Century City and beyond" (*City of Los Angeles v. Playboy Gangster Crips* 1987d). The crime was seeping out of Cadillac-Corning north toward more affluent areas.

But the pockets of wealth were also the drug dealers' biggest clients (Davis 2006, 280). An officer who grew up and later worked in the area explained in an interview that Cadillac-Corning, located about a mile south of Beverly Hills, was the preferred drive-through drug market of affluent whites. Upper-class white people had a source nearby that they felt comfortable patronizing. In a court declaration, an officer regretfully described the misperceptions held by drug buyers: "They get lulled into a false sense of security, somehow thinking it's safer to buy here on Corning Street than on Figueroa. . . . All kinds of people go into that neighborhood to buy drugs. A lot of middle and upper class people. All ages, races, ethnic backgrounds, from every profession, too" (*City of Los Angeles v. Playboy Gangster Crips* 1987a).

Media covered a number of murders that occurred in Cadillac-Corning in the 1980s. In court, police officers discussed several of these shootings. Attention was not equally distributed among cases. News reports and court documents repeatedly recount the story of a white teenager on a motorcycle murdered by the PBGs after a drug deal gone bad. The drug seller thought he had been given less money than the agreed upon amount. He signaled a partner at the end of the block who shot the buyer to death.

A *Los Angeles Times* article, entitled, "Drug-Peddling Street Gang Holds Neighborhood in Fear" mentioned only two murders. One was the murder of a 14-year-old, who the report emphasized was a gang member. The other murder covered was that of the white youth on the motorcycle: "Drug buyers have also been robbed, raped or gunned down, authorities say. In late 1986, a 16-year-old involved in a business misunderstanding with a Playboy Gangster drug dealer was killed by a lookout who, upon receiving a signal, stepped out of an apartment building and fired a gun as the youth drove off on his motorcycle" (Feldman 1987c).

An officer explained the case in his court testimony, "We've had incidents where customers try to rip off the dealer but by the time they reach the end of the street, the lookout's been notified and the lookout will jump out with a gun and shoot the customer. We had the guy on the motorcycle who bought some dope with a buddy on his back" (*City of Los Angeles v. Playboy Gangster Crips* 1987d). In court, officers keep returning to the murder of the young white male on the motorcycle. They mention all of the other murders, including the murders of children from Cadillac-corning, briefly, and only one time for each case. The motorcycle murder is also the only case in which they mentioned the race of the victim. For example, an officer testified, "If they think there's a rip off, a lookout is signaled and he will shoot the customer or problem person before he reaches the end of the block. That happened about a year ago with a 16 year old white kid on a motorcycle" (*City of Los Angeles v. Playboy Gangster Crips* 1987d). In his testimony, another officer felt it necessary to clarify that the young white man was not gang involved, "On October 5, 1986, at approximately 11:40 P.M., Jeremy Steven Heading, a 16 year old white male, was also murdered near the corner of Corning Street and Guthrie Avenue. . . . The victim had no known gang affiliation but was only in the neighborhood to purchase rock cocaine" (*City of Los Angeles v. Playboy Gangster Crips* 1987f).

John remembered the case of the 16-year-old white male more vividly than any other. In our interview it was the only specific murder that he mentioned, "A white kid one year was murdered right at the end of the corner at the end of Corning. It was a mistake we found out. They thought he'd been cheated on his money and he wasn't." John went on to explain that gang violence did not become a priority until violence reached beyond low-income neighborhoods of color,

> Well, before that started no one was caring about gangs. Up until that point and our resources were very little. It was kind of a token thing. It was a political thing. The elected officials saying, "I'm going to go after the gangs." But you know what? Virtually all of the community really didn't still care about it because it was confined to the lower-income neighborhoods. Nobody was being killed in—no white people were being killed.

John clarified that he did not mean that the police did not care; rather, it was the politicians and community members. The people who doled out resources and the constituents that provided mass support did not feel touched by the violence. Cadillac-Corning changed that. Councilmen Zev Yaroslavsky wrote to the city attorney at the time, James Hahn, about the

PBGs' presence in Cadillac-Corning: "The gang activity in this community has had a very negative effect upon the neighbors in bordering communities" (Office of Los Angeles City Councilman Zev Yaroslavsky 1987).

In an interview with the *Los Angeles Times*, Hahn clarified that the purpose of the injunction was not to alleviate violence but to shift responsibility: "Maybe it's pushed off to somewhere else, but we're going to keep following that phantom around the city until we have enough resources to keep it on the move and maybe move it out completely" (*Los Angeles Times* 1993).

City prosecutors and the LAPD did not strategically pick the Cadillac-Corning neighborhood or the Playboy Gangster Crips gang from the rest of the city. Rather, the city prosecutors who drafted the injunction worked in the West Los Angeles area. Cadillac-Corning was singled out as a threatening space within West Los Angeles. The final gang injunction itself does not mention race explicitly. It simply lists names, locations, and prohibited behavior. Nonetheless, unequivocally racist ideas about black youth, morality, intelligence, and family life are woven throughout the interviews, primary documents, and court proceedings in which authorities record their observations and argue for the injunction. Officers and city prosecutors built the injunction off of racial stereotypes about black families and youth, fear of young black men, and the perceived threat they posed to surrounding areas. In the 20-year period prior to the injunction, Cadillac-Corning underwent a significant demographic change from a middle-class white Jewish area to a solidly black and working-class neighborhood. As the number of black families swelled, so did the police presence and the panic of white neighbors. For years, wealthier whites from nearby neighborhoods had enjoyed Cadillac-Corning as a convenient drug market. However, Cadillac-Corning garnered attention after several white drug patrons were robbed and one was murdered. Law enforcement was not concerned with gangs per se, which is a form of social organization that has spanned time, place, race, and ethnicity. Rather, police and city prosecutors were concerned with black youth running a drug business in close proximity to affluent white neighborhoods. Police and city prosecutors designed a policy to contain black youth within Cadillac-Corning's apartments or push them out of the neighborhood altogether. In the final injunction document, the term "gang" is really a reference to black men.

FROM THE CORNER TO THE COURTROOM

With all of the information they had gathered, the prosecutors had to sit down and write the injunction. First, they defined the modern street gang as "a group of individuals who associate together for a number of purposes." Those purposes include the "sale of narcotics; commission of thefts, burglaries, and robberies; occupation of territory; and acquisition of 'status' and 'power' through group-concerted action and intimidation" (*People v. Playboy Gangster Crips* 1987).

City prosecutors argued in court documents that a street gang constitutes an "unincorporated association" because it meets the following criteria: "(1) a group whose members share a common purpose, and (2) who function under a common name under circumstances where fairness requires that the group be recognized as a legal entity" (*People v. Playboy Gangster Crips* 1987). As an unincorporated association, gangs as organizations are held liable for the actions of their members. The actions of individual members, in turn, are assumed to advance the illegal profit-generating activities of the gang. Prosecutors and police argued that prosecuting the gang as a unit rather than a collection of individuals was absolutely necessary to disrupt the communication network and coordinated business operations.

Many groups fit this description yet are not prosecuted as unincorporated associations, including fraternities, conspiring Enron executives, and corrupt police. The Los Angeles Sheriff's Department admits they have groups of deputies that have a collective name, group tattoos, and an internal hierarchy through which deputies advance by brutalizing jail inmates and civilians on the street. The most notorious of these sheriff gangs is the Jump Out Boys. Instead of using the term "gang," however, the Sheriff's Department refers to them as "cliques." One member of a sheriff's clique called the Vikings was a top contender in the most recent race for Los Angeles County Sheriff. No white supremacist groups have gang injunctions, despite Southern California's concentration of white supremacist activity. Furthermore, while the predominantly Latino motorcycle group the Mongols is enjoined from wearing their logo, the Hells Angels remain unrestrained.

The proposed injunction prohibited alleged gang members from engaging in otherwise legal activity in the area covered by the injunction on the grounds that it was a public nuisance under civil law. City prosecutors argued in the memorandum that

> it is the contention of the People that all of these acts, taken together, constitute a public nuisance as defined in Civil Code sections 3479 and 3480, in that these acts are injurious to health, or offensive to the senses, or obstruct the free use of property so as to interfere with the comfortable enjoyment of life and property of an entire community or neighborhood, as well as by a considerable number of persons. (*People v. Playboy Gangster Crips* 1987)

City prosecutors argued that the actions of alleged gang members were "injurious to health, or offensive to the senses" and obstructed "the free use of property" (*People v. Playboy Gangster Crips* 1987). They claimed that the public nuisance posed by gang members justified the restriction of constitutional rights. For example, the prosecutors sought to prohibit alleged gang members from congregating in groups of two or more and from loitering for more than five minutes. Restrictions on association would upset communication and drug solicitation in Cadillac-Corning. Alleged gang members who did not live in Cadillac-Corning would not be allowed into the neighborhood. For those who did live or work in Cadillac-Corning, "24 hours would be allowed to obtain letters of residence or employment." Of the Fifth Amendment right to travel, the court memorandum read, "The right of every American to come and to go must frequently, in the face of sudden danger, be temporarily limited or suspended" (*People v. Playboy Gangster Crips* 1987). Of course, there is nothing temporary about gang injunctions since most do not have an expiration date but, instead, are indefinite.

Up until 2007, there was no exit process that allowed one to be removed from a gang injunction if they could prove they were no longer involved in a gang or had been wrongly added (Vannoy 2009, 285). As of 2012, only nine removal petitions had been granted (Office of the City Attorney of Los Angeles 2012). The most common reason for rejected petitions was "Recent contact evidencing gang related activity" (Office of the City Attorney of Los Angeles 2012). Police contact, not conviction or even arrest. The removal process takes six to nine months and requires that petitioners do not have law enforcement contact for two years prior, a feat that is nearly impossible considering that injunctions allow law enforcement to maintain contact with those who are enjoined.

Cadillac-Corning was, and remains, a neighborhood predominantly composed of closely spaced two- and three-story apartment buildings interspersed with single-family homes. Police complained that suspects often escaped pursuit through routes between apartment buildings and by using objects to boost themselves out of windows and over fences. Consequently, the proposed injunction stated that alleged gang members were prohibited from climbing trees and fences or positioning milk crates and cinder blocks under windows or near fences. Within the injunction area, alleged gang members were not allowed to carry binoculars, pagers, cell phones, or flashlights. These were considered contraband that a lookout would carry. They were also prohibited from standing on balconies or rooftops where they could act as lookouts and warn others about approaching police. Black youth on bikes were targeted because authorities concluded that they were either acting as lookouts or moving drugs. In an interview, John explained that the injunction gave an officer the authority to say, "You're on a bicycle with a pager. You're going to jail." Instead of an undercover officer busting one person for selling drugs, the injunction allowed a uniformed officer to make large sweeps.

The injunction identified a variety of actions that were "precursors" to the ultimate crimes of drug dealing and violence. The goal was to arrest alleged gang members before they did anything technically illegal. In the spirit of predictive policing, law enforcement was concerned with what alleged gang members might do rather than acts they already committed. John laid out the problem and his proposed solution in his declaration to the court: "If, for example, police officers were able to stop and detain gang members before they dealt their drugs to be sure they are not in possession of any contraband, then law enforcement would be able to slow down and interfere with the drug dealing" (*City of Los Angeles v. Playboy Gangster Crips* 1987e).

Let us take a moment here to remember the neighborhood context. In the two decades before the injunction, Cadillac-Corning changed from a predominantly white area to one that was predominantly African American. The neighborhoods surrounding Cadillac-Corning were still overwhelmingly white and upper-middle class. Authorities were not targeting alleged gang members just anywhere—they were targeting them in this neighborhood in particular. John clarified in an interview how important the politics of geography are to the criminalizing effect of the injunction:

> This little crime of trespassing would be nothing in the court out of context but in the context of what's going on in the community, it's a big crime. . . . We would go in and say, "He's got a suspended license but, your honor, *he's this person in this neighborhood.*" So when somebody would get a $300 fine [elsewhere], you'd get a $3000 fine for a suspended license. We'd literally get 90, 120 days in jail. (emphasis added)

Relatively progressive groups trusted authorities' use of the injunction. The president of the Los Angeles chapter of National Association for the Advancement of Colored People said he supported the Cadillac-Corning injunction because he believed it would "return the community back to the people" (Feldman 1987a). He further stated to the *Los Angeles Times* that authorities adequately assured him that the injunction would only be used to target a small group of hard-core gang members, which is the same line prosecutors and police give the community today.

The staff attorney from the American Civil Liberties Union (ACLU) who argued against the case had a different perspective on the proposed injunction, stating to the media, "This is the first time that I would characterize anything going on in the City of Los Angeles as coming close to a police state" (Feldman 1987a). The ACLU challenged the injunction on the grounds that the injunction left alleged gang members without basic legal protections. The ACLU claimed several of the provisions were unconstitutional, such as the requirement that visitors to alleged gang members' residences had to stay longer than 10 minutes. (Visits shorter than 10 minutes were considered prospective drug deals.) The result was three months of court appearances, which attracted groups of spectators and was covered extensively in local and national news.

In an interview, the ACLU staff attorney on the case remembered that she found it unfair that Cadillac-Corning was targeted: "The issue was not that it was such a terrible neighborhood. But it was close to more prosperous neighborhoods. That was the point of it." The ACLU staff attorney further believed that the civil process was biased against defendants. "It was not a fact-based case. It was a weird case because I did not have clients. I was defending the constitutional rights of the John Does. Why wouldn't you circumvent the criminal process if you could?"

During his consideration of the injunction, the Los Angeles Superior Court judge presiding over the case expressed skepticism that civil sanctions would work, considering that more severe criminal sanctions had been ineffective against the PBGs (Feldman 1987b). He criticized the use of civil sanctions on the basis that they would be time-consuming and result in a maximum jail sentence of only five days. The judge advised the City Attorney's Office to file criminal charges against alleged gang members instead. John explained in an interview, however, that there were benefits to a civil, rather than criminal, injunction: "When a gang member comes in on a gang injunction they don't have a right to council. They don't have a right to a jury trial. They don't have the right to a speedy—all of those rights that we have to deal with, which I respect. I had a tool that gave me all of these advantages. Why give the defendant back so much stuff?" The gang injunction developed a two-tiered criminal justice system in Los Angeles in which people of color in stigmatized neighborhoods could be disproportionately targeted and punished for behavior considered innocuous in any other context. The use of the civil court system further stacked the odds against defendants.

The final injunction prohibited gang members from doing the following: murder, robbery, rape, drug dealing, drug solicitations, shootings, burglary, theft, knifings, intimidation of residents, public drunkenness, assaults, weapons possession, trespassing, obstruction of pedestrian traffic, littering, vandalism, verbal abuse, public nudity, child abuse, witness intimidation, reckless driving, excessive noise, and public urination or defecation (Office of the City Attorney of Los Angeles 1987). The judge struck down the many of the restrictions in the original court order as unconstitutionally overreaching and "too broad to grant," including a 7:00 P.M. to 7:00 A.M. curfew for enjoined youth, a prohibition against congregating in groups of two or more, a ban on wearing gang-related colors, requiring visitors to enjoined residences stay longer than 10 minutes, and loitering in public for more than five minutes (Feldman 1987a).

John was largely dissatisfied with the final injunction because it prohibited illegal behavior only. Although many of the prohibitions sought by prosecutors were thrown off the Cadillac-Corning injunction, they were drawn on for inclusion in later injunctions. Many of the restrictions the judge opposed in 1987 are standard parts of gang injunctions today. For example, in 1993, the same prosecutors that wrote the Cadillac-Corning injunction attained an injunction against the Blythe Street Gang. The Blythe Street injunction included (but was not limited to) prohibitions against possessing baseball bats, metal pipes, glass bottles, chains, rocks, screwdrivers, marbles, razors, large metal buckets, whistles, flashlights, markers, car parts without written proof of purchase, and wearing pagers in places open to public view. Approaching vehicles, climbing trees, standing on buildings, and associating with alleged gang members was also prohibited (*People v. Blythe Street Gang* 1993).

In 1995, the Sixth District Court of Appeals ruled that under public nuisance law only criminal conduct could be prohibited. According to the ruling, since standing in public space and wearing certain colors were not criminal conduct, they could not be prohibited in the injunction. In 1997, however, the California Supreme Court overturned the 1995 decision, thus upholding key noncriminal provisions in gang injunctions, including the nonassociation prohibition (*People ex rel. Gallo v. Acuna* 1997). After the 1997 decision, injunctions with these prohibitions were once again routinely implemented.

The injunction had effects even when prosecutions were not pursued. City prosecutors announced the times and places that they would be serving alleged gang members to attract media and residents. During his testimony in a later court case, the LAPD officer in charge of coordinating enforcement efforts discussed the Cadillac-Corning injunction's informal effects: "Interestingly enough, we didn't really arrest that many people on the injunction but there was something about the public notification to the gang and the community meetings that just had a tremendous effect in reducing their criminal activities" (*People v. Blythe St. Gang* 1993). Perhaps the biggest "success" of the injunction was that it terrorized people into fleeing public space and, sometimes, the neighborhood.

John mentioned another success to me, regarding property values: "The Realtors were—and by the way, this was at a point when real estate in the city was the highest ever—and in Corning nobody could buy a house or sell a house. It was like the way the whole country is now. Then Realtors were saying, 'Oh, we're seeing a change. Property values are going up and the street is looking better.'"

The injunction prohibitions eventually invaded private space, too. When authorities chased people, they often retreated into friends' apartments. In later injunctions, prosecutors attained court orders stating that an alleged gang member could not be in another's residence without written permission. The order allowed police to enter and remove people from apartment units.

In summary, the injunction was shaped, first, by ethnography conducted by prosecutors and police. City prosecutors decided which activities to prohibit from their meticulous observation of the neighborhood's black youth. They were primarily interested, not in criminal activities, but in the routine behavior of black youth that could lead to crimes. They targeted actions like hanging out, riding a bike, and carrying tools, which the ACLU and the presiding judge considered unconstitutionally broad. Although some prohibitions were thrown out, they later returned to injunctions. The prohibitions and protocols, laced with racial control, set forth in the Cadillac-Corning injunction built the path for future injunctions. The injunction was then shaped by the interplay in court proceedings. The prosecutors, police officers, neighborhood context, and court struggle that created the path are buried in archives. But what they set in motion is detrimental to youth of color in Los Angeles more than two decades later.

THE INJUNCTION IS INSTITUTIONALIZED

Chapter 5 of this book is dedicated to the Glendale Corridor Gang Injunction, implemented in a low-crime, rapidly gentrifying part of Los Angeles. In the declarations for the proposed injunction an officer stated, "Street sales are largely a thing of the past. Most narco sales now are to customers they know" (*People v. Big Top Locos* 2013d). The original point of injunctions—to disrupt drug businesses—is now obsolete in its purpose. Nonetheless, gang injunctions have become a primary standardized policy for police and city prosecutors. Each new injunction is a slightly altered boilerplate version of previous injunctions, regardless of the community on which they are levied. In an interview, a current Los Angeles Gang Unit prosecutor who has worked on over a dozen injunctions described the modern day process:

When I came in, other people had invented gang injunctions, late eighties, early nineties. About a half dozen agencies around the state were all working on it. So the concept existed via prosecutors kind of stumbling around in civil court, fish out of water. And they were kind of like custom-making every single injunction. Big, huge process. . . . The way I like to say it is, Henry Ford didn't invent the model of the car, but he made it so he could mass produce it. And we've had a bunch of people here with no civil experience at all, you know, step in and just knock off injunctions and take about a year to do it, which is a world of difference than the nineties. . . . I don't talk to civilians about gang injunctions. I talk to gang unit cops and gang prosecutors. . . . If you tell a civilian that with a gang injunction, someone can't sit with their friend on a front porch, they're going to say, "Wow, that's terrible." Gang injunctions are harsh—I don't apologize for that.

Near the end of our interview, John argued that the gang injunction was not intended to be such a blunt, widely used policy celebrated by the gang prosecutor quoted above. "It became a mass factory. Let's stamp out gang injunctions to give cops the chance to stop anybody for any reason." He leaned his elbows on his desk, his tone slipping from a nostalgic excitement to one resigned and serious. "They're proud of the fact that they can advertise, you know, the City Attorney, there were 55 gang injunctions or 60, whatever. It will have an effect. It will stop the gang in the sense that it will disrupt everything. . . . If that's the standard, if you walk next to a gang member, then you are now part of the injunction." He shakes his head slightly and adds, "That's not what my baby was about."

The now-naturalized classification systems of gang membership and target areas began with specific racial struggles in particular geographies during a contentious historical moment. The gang injunction was not implemented in the area with the most gang activity, assaults, or murders. Rather, it was instituted where borders separating black and white, wealthy and working class were becoming porous. The injunction and accompanying police crackdown came to Cadillac-Corning after school desegregation, housing development, and neighborhood racial change. To specifically tailor the injunction to control the movement of black youth and upset the Playboy Gangster Crips' drug operation, police and city prosecutors conducted an in-depth study of the Cadillac-Corning neighborhood.

In an early version of broken windows policing, they sought to control black youth through the prohibition of precursors to crime—mundane behavior that is legal outside of the context of the target neighborhood and criminalized people. Although the initial injunction targeted only illegal behavior, in practice a range of legal behavior was criminalized. Later, in the 1990s and 2000s, injunctions expanded to officially prohibit a broad swath of noncriminal acts, giving police discretion to stop, detain, and arrest people based on their appearance, assumptions about what they might do, and their mere presence in a geographical area. Thus, gang injunctions provide police and prosecutors with the legal discretion to carry out extralegal control and repression. The development of gang injunctions is the development of a dual system of criminal justice in which low-income urban people of color are targeted and given harsh punishment for things that are considered innocuous outside of stigmatized neighborhoods and the criminalized status of gang membership. Gang injunctions are reflective of a legal system designed to maintain racial boundaries without explicit mention of race.

Although race politics are central to authorities' observations and interpretation of a street gang, any references to race were sanitized out of the legal definition. In the years since the Cadillac-Corning injunction, a protocol has been developed to streamline the implementation of gang injunctions. In the process, the authors of the Cadillac-Corning injunction were erased, the neighborhood's role was forgotten, and the "gang membership" label was naturalized as a stand-in for explicit racial references. Since the first injunction, the powerful label of "gang member" has evolved such that it is used to justify violent state action. It is a status that sparks fear in the general public. Police, policy makers, and media outlets constantly exploit the "gang membership" label in a way that legitimizes repression. For example, on a regular basis major newspapers and news channels will report some version of the headline, "Police Shoot Gang Member." Because the person is an alleged gang member no more questions are asked—regarding the context of the shooting, how the police and media are certain the person was a gang member, and why it is even relevant. The dehumanized view of alleged gang members influences media representations and everyday citizen interactions with black and Latino youth. The gang injunction successfully criminalized alleged gang membership as a separate social class (Davis 2006, 278).

The war on gangs is a primary reason that California's massive system of incarceration and surveillance continues to balloon. Whether injunctions are used to wage a war on gangs, drugs, or art, it all ends up being a war on LA's least powerful communities. The disproportionate effect of gang injunctions on people of color means that gang injunctions are working the way they are supposed to. It is a problem at the base of the idea of the injunction, not simply a blemish to be administratively corrected.

The legacy of the injunction is still imprinted on the reputation of and policing tactics in Cadillac-Corning more than 20 years later. The practice of building gates at the end of alleyways to preclude getaway routes is still standard. Police continue to target youth on bicycles as suspected lookouts for the drug business. Injunctions go hand in hand with the rise of the broken windows theory of policing and law enforcement concern with what people might do—or look like they might do—rather than with what acts people have actually committed. The legacy of stigmatization that began in the 1960s, and was cemented by the gang injunction in the 1980s, continued into the 1990s with the arrival of police-community partnerships to target blight. Cadillac-Corning was and, in many ways, still is an abrupt dividing line in which authorities attempt to contain people of color. The current state of policing in Cadillac-Corning centers on police-community partnerships. Through partnerships, the broken windows theory has seeped into popular consciousness. The neighborhood stigmatization inspires residents in surrounding areas to use the broken windows framework in a panic over what they believe to be small signs of disorder and an impending criminal invasion.

CHAPTER 4

The Chaos of Upstanding Citizens

DISORDERLY COMMUNITY PARTNERS AND BROKEN WINDOWS POLICING

LET US CATCH UP by returning to the beginning of this book. Remember, it is 2012 in Los Angeles; there is a neon pink sunset and nine officers of the law at my back gate. Officially there is no Cadillac-Corning anymore. As of 2003 the neighborhood is La Cienega Heights. A local community group voted to change the name as part of LA City's neighborhood naming initiative. I have been regularly attending community meetings on public safety with the community group, business and homeowners associations, city prosecutors, and the police.

There are several points of potential danger that the community group is consistently concerned about. The group has the same concerns every meeting. For example, apartment renters are a recurring threat. One community group member commented, "I have been in the neighborhood for three years. I own two buildings. I believe that it is up to landlords to get rid of the neighborhood's crime problem. Landlords need to raise rents and renovate their buildings to get rid of the riffraff. If any other landlords are interested, talk to me after the meeting about getting together. Thank you." The predominantly white, home-owning group of residents was also concerned about the neighborhood's black youth. "They have no respect for cars or anything else. They will not move for cars that come into the intersection. The other day, a car clipped one of the kids. The driver was black, the kid on the skateboard was also black, so they laughed it off. I fear that if the driver had been another color it would not have been settled so easily."

Hamilton High School students are also a reliable topic. Today, Hamilton is essentially a two-track school. The campus consists of the "original school" and two magnets. The two magnets have larger percentages of white students, higher test scores, and better college attendance rates than the predominantly black and Latino original school. Many of the black and Latino students live in Cadillac-Corning. The policing of the youth of color who walk from Cadillac-Corning to Hamilton has been expanded and refined. The Neighborhood Council outfitted the Hamilton High School security agents, the Los Angeles Unified School District Police Department officer, and the assistant principal with cell phones. The phones provide "the community" with access to the various punitive entities at Hamilton High, as the meeting facilitator explained:

> Every day in the morning and afternoon, Hamilton students flood the community. Hamilton wants to expand the safe zone because they have liability issues. We want to keep the community safe from some of the knuckleheads that may be in the groups of students. The purpose of the phones is to call in, not for calling out. We have a list of numbers. If anyone sees anything out of the ordinary, they can call and report it.

The lightning-rod issues from the 1960s—apartment development and regulating the racial threat to bordering neighborhoods—survive. The ripple effects of piecemeal midcentury changes in housing development, transportation, and enrollment at the local high school are imprinted on the physical layout and social makeup of the neighborhood today. The majority of the firepower for the 64-square-mile West Division of the LAPD is concentrated within the boundaries of Cadillac-Corning. The local council office assigns a field deputy to drive though the streets and alleyways of the neighborhood daily to address graffiti. Local media reinforces the stigmatization of the neighborhood by referring to Cadillac-Corning as a "tough pocket" that the good forces of gentrification have not been able to "revitalize" (Blankstein and Gencer 2006).

Of all the threats discussed in the meetings, the targeting of street vendors crystallizes how residents in community groups define danger, community, the role of the police, and their relationship to local government. Community group members have adopted the broken windows ideology and used it for their own ends in attempts to oppose street vending in their area. Despite official attempts to diminish the expectations of community group members, residents in community groups have utilized the broken windows theory to portray vending as a harbinger of crime. Armed with this claim, community groups demand specific action and resources from the police. Although the police have the badge and the gun, wealthy, politically well connected citizens wield myriad forms of subtle power.

THE "COMMUNITY" IN COMMUNITY PARTNERSHIPS AND BROKEN WINDOWS POLICING

Throughout the early and mid-20th century, police in American cities strove to keep their distance from the neighborhoods they policed (Garland 2001). Detachment was not only intended as an antidote to rampant corruption but also as a way to shield departments from public scrutiny. Professionalization gave the appearance that policing could be scientifically efficient and apolitical (Lyons 1999). However, social unrest, high-profile cases of police brutality, and consistently high crime rates were a few factors that sparked misgivings about professionalized policing in the 1970s.

Two prominent models that emerged, broken windows policing and community policing, entail distinct roles for community members and law enforcement. Community policing involves cooperation between police and residents in the development of crime prevention strategies. Broken windows policing places emphasis on order maintenance by officers with community members in a supporting role. Despite the traditional theoretical differences in the two paradigms, in practice many urban police forces implement both simultaneously (DeMichele and Kraska 2001).

Police departments across the country have turned to community policing measures in the realization that informal social control exercised through everyday relationships and institutions is more effective than legal sanctions (Garland 2001). When I use the term "community partnerships" I refer to programs that bring the police, select residents, and at times, other relevant government agencies together to develop problem-solving projects as a fear reduction and crime prevention strategy. There are several directions community partnerships can take and a variety of tensions and contradictory elements that can arise in the implementation of community policing. Some researchers view community policing programs as a potential challenge to the hard-line antidemocratic nature of the broken windows model (Trojanowicz and Bucqueroux 1990; Herbert 2001). Critical scholars, however, argue that community policing is a top-down, rather than collaborative, endeavor in which the police use community groups for their own purposes (Crawford 1997; Garland 2001).

Unlike community policing, broken windows (also called order maintenance or zero-tolerance policing) implies a more passive role for residents, who are viewed as being unable to battle disorder in their neighborhoods (Herbert 2001). Proponents of the broken windows theory argue that the accumulation of small acts of disorder creates an environment conducive to serious crimes like robbery or assault. Disorder causes a general feeling of fear to which law-abiders react by fleeing into their homes or to more orderly gated estates. Conversely, the "wrong" kinds of people are supposedly attracted to disorderly areas because they are seen as easy places to commit crimes. The concept of disorder is necessarily vague and indefinitely expansive, allowing for ample police discretion. A few signs of so-called physical and social disorder are litter, graffiti, the presence of truants, loiterers, people who are homeless, and street vendors (Parenti 2001). Preventative policing grants the police discretion to target signs of disorder in order to prevent the escalation to violent crime (Wilson and Kelling 1982; Bratton and Malinowski 2008). Despite official race neutrality in the language of the broken windows theory, definitions of disorder are laced with implications about race, class, and public space (Stewart 1998; Roberts 1999). The practice of broken windows policing relies on a racial ideology that connects the dark/foreign other to unpredictable chaos and criminality. The disorderly people targeted by police are overwhelmingly lower-class, black, and Latino, who are using public space.

Researchers have extensively debated the theoretical and empirical merit of the disorder-crime continuum (Harcourt 2001; Sampson and

Raudenbush 2004; Xu, Fiedler, and Flaming 2005) and the effects of order maintenance policing on public life, informal economies, arrests patterns, and fear of crime (Stewart 1998; Duneier 2001; Parenti 2001; Hinkle and Weisburd 2008; Jang, Hoover, and Lawton 2008). Robert Trojanowicz and Bonnie Bucqueroux (1990) contend that order maintenance policing can effectively reduce fear of crime. Joshua C. Hinkle and David Weisburd (2008), however, find that the visible police intervention launched to restore order can decrease general feelings of safety. Mike Davis (2002, 8) and Adam Crawford (1997, 271) maintain that, rather than increasing feelings of safety, the constant monitoring of disorder and danger "paradoxically generate[s] radical insecurity," which can "institutionalize anxiety" in middle-class urban residents. Residents in turn demand greater responsiveness from both public and private agents of security. However, just because authorities have the discretion to act on something does not mean they will. It is the difference between what broken windows allows police to do and what it would obligate that the police do. Order maintenance means that "broad criminal laws . . . allow the police to take people off the streets because they look suspicious" (Harcourt 2001, 128). The police have broad discretion to remove people deemed undesirable. Whether and how they respond to disorder is contingent on multiple extralegal factors.

Despite distinct roles for residents and officers as an ideal type, community policing programs can be made compatible with the broken windows theory through an emphasis on informal social control, moral binaries, and the construction of an exclusive community (DeMichele and Kraska 2001; Herbert 2001). Under a circular logic, the degeneration of community is both the cause and the result of crime (Crawford 1997). Crime and disorder cause law-abiding people to retreat into their homes in fear. The lack of interaction breeds yet more fear, causing people to become further detached. Thus, strengthening community is both a means and an end (Sasson 1995). Compared to the ideal of community policing, residents are more limited in their actions under the broken windows policing model. Properly behaved residents are to upkeep their property, observe disorderly others, and alert officers to signs of disorder. Fear is reduced, order restored, and community is built through the formal and informal social control of an Other.

VENDORS AS THE BROKEN
WINDOW: COMMUNITY GROUPS
AND HARM ARGUMENTS

In a document addressed to the captain of the West Los Angeles Police Department (WLAPD) in June 2005, the La Cienega Heights (LACH) Community Group articulated their concerns about the broken windows approach, saying, "We are a community seeking to revitalize its livability and image. We have truly bought into Chief [William] Bratton's broken windows credo and believe that a neighborhood that looks neglected invites crime and deviant behavior."

Three years later, in the spring of 2008, residents of La Cienega Heights who attended community meetings had recent violence on their minds. During 10 days in late March and early April, three shootings, one resulting in a fatality, occurred in the area. It was rumored that the shootings were gang related. Frustrated, anxious people filled the cafeterias of the local schools after work to demand answers. How could they let this happen? What were they planning to do to protect "law-abiding" residents? The WLAPD captain and other uniformed officers sat in a panel at the front of the room with the neighborhood prosecutor from the City Attorney's Office and a detective in a charcoal gray suit. They repeatedly assured everyone that they were making progress on the case. The criminals would be arrested and punished. Resources were going to be poured into the neighborhood.

There was one topic that popped up in all of the open question sessions at the end of each meeting. Laura, a member of the LACH Community Group, asked the newly assigned senior lead officer, Angela, what the WLAPD planned to do about the persistence of illegal vendors:

LAURA: Summer is coming, during which the neighborhood will be invaded by vendors. It doesn't frame the neighborhood well.

ANGELA: I just shooed away some vendors by the Bank of America. Dealing with the vendors is like mowing the lawn. If you don't stay on top of it, they grow back thicker. But they are not a very high priority. Burglaries are picking up and all crime picks up in the summer, including gang activity.

LAURA: They may not just be selling wares. They observe, they tip off. It's the broken windows theory.

ANGELA: It is very much a blight on society. It is very much a broken windows problem. If you can send me the information on where they are and when—times are very important—I can forward the information onto patrol for them to take care of.

Laura's statement exemplifies how community groups considered vendors to be outside elements that assaulted the community. This instance is just one of many examples in which residents in community groups demonstrated an awareness of the broken windows theory of crime, however misconstrued, that the LAPD formally espoused. The LACH Community Group had adopted the paradigm of broken windows. It shaped their work and their interaction with local government services. Residents essentially reversed broken windows logic. Rather than identifying vending as a cause of disorder that could lead to murder, their focus on vending was sparked by a murder. The leap from murder to vendors was mediated by fuzzy concepts like "blight" that were used with such frequency they came to encompass an increasingly broad range of people, activities, and spaces. Laura's interaction with Angela also highlights the tension between the LAPD's broken windows ideology, the daily practice of police work, and the department's attempt to institute community policing.

Vending took a variety of forms in the neighborhood. After more than a year and a half, I barely noticed the horn that announced the arrival of the Latino produce vendor in front of my house anywhere from two to five times a day. The tune to the first couple lines of "La Cucaracha" blared through the static of a loudspeaker attached to the top of the white truck. The broken horn could not play the full first two lines of the song, though. Instead, the music spiked, dipped, and broke up before trailing off limply. Another, older Latino vendor parked his produce truck at the same spot every day, remaining stationary to sell products. Two ice cream trucks played lullabies as they lumbered up and down the neighborhood's narrow streets. Additionally, a young Latino man with small bells dangling from the handle of a push cart sold ice cream and pork rinds throughout the day. Around sunset a middle-aged Latina pushing a cart shouted out her product, "taaaamaaaales!" During the spring and summer a man set up a fruit stand at a busy four-way stop.

In hopes of eradicating vending from the neighborhood, community groups tried to connect vendors to danger from a number of angles. Bernard Harcourt (2001, 194) argues that the disorder–crime nexus hinges on "harm arguments" that flourish in political and legal debates. Those who deploy harm arguments contend that certain actions are harmful rather than simply annoying, morally offensive, or aesthetically objectionable. Harcourt takes loitering as one example. Throughout the 1960s and 1970s, antiloitering ordinances prohibited public idleness insofar as it posed a nuisance to others. With the rise of the broken windows theory, policy makers and law enforcement have justified similar ordinances by arguing that loitering is a broken window that attracts crime, such as gang activity (Harcourt 2001). Loiterers, homeless people, unattended youth, and so on, are deemed responsible for the potential neighborhood spiral into crime and urban decay. Thus loitering is transformed from an inconvenience to disorderly and harmful behavior that justifies police intervention.

At first, community groups complained that vendors were an annoyance. The LACH Community Group initially argued that their quality of life was being affected through small but compounding infractions. They alleged that noise pollution from vendors' horns and bells, congregation of crowds around the trucks, and litter created a feeling of disorder that made them generally fearful as well as lowered property values. In response, police argued that quality-of-life offenses are extremely difficult to catch as they are happening. For example, to cite a vendor for noise pollution, the police would have to monitor vendors and measure the decibels of their horns.

After they failed to extract an enforcement response, the community group turned to harm arguments that more forcefully associated vendors with harm. For example, community group members claimed that the graffiti on vending trucks constituted a visual blight that attracted violent crime. Furthermore, the LACH Community Group complained that the vendors constituted a health risk to the community. They demanded coordination between the WLAPD and the Los Angeles County Health Department to shut down the carts and confiscate their goods for selling food in subgrade conditions. Again, police responded that they did not have the personnel to launch a coordinated operation. The LACH

Community Group also complained that the undocumented immigration status of many vendors indicated that they were not taxed or properly licensed. Community group members argued that vendors further undercut taxed and licensed businesses when they pulled customers away. Officers claimed that they would target illegal vendors if businesses filed complaints. On the contrary, several businesses actually protected vendors by renting out space to them.

Finally, community group members' requests became structured around increasingly explicit connections between vendors and danger through claims that vendors were themselves perpetrators of criminal activities. At the end of 2008, LACH Community Group members began telling authorities they had reason to believe that one of the vendors started to sell marijuana and other drugs as well as food. One recurring story involved an ice cream man who was caught a few years previously selling toy guns near the elementary school. At times, people said he was also selling pellet guns, fireworks, or cigarettes. More important than the details of the story was the function of the narrative. It was a documented example that community group members could use as leverage against those who were unconvinced by their harm arguments. The story explicitly connected the vendor with the predation of children as justification for the aggressive eradication of all vendors. Either you were invested in the antivending crusade or you sided with violent gang members, child predators, and drug dealers.

Community groups marshaled broken windows arguments to prompt action from various local government agents. Community groups began with complaints that vendors brought disorder into the physical environment and that police should have addressed annoyances that affected their quality of life. They then sought other local government agencies to regulate and enforce various violations. Eventually, they returned to appeals to law enforcement, but this time through the lens of social disorder and the explicit connection of vendors to criminal behavior. Community group members increasingly linked vendors to active predation because appeals through broken windows logic did not convince authorities. A deconstruction of harm arguments highlights the ambiguity involved in locating vendors on the disorder-crime continuum. A lot of work goes into the separation of disorderly deviants and orderly law-abiders. Daily life defies clean categorization. There is not just one form of disorder. Accordingly, part of defining disorder is deciding who is supposed to restore order.

Ironically, the ever-expanding scope of harm arguments complicated an official law enforcement response because different harm arguments implied the jurisdiction of very different agencies. There was no one institution to address vending. Despite all of the institutional representatives who met in community partnerships, the process to report vendors was unclear. At times vending violated health codes. In some situations, vending qualified as an illegal activity. Community group members felt they held up their half of community policing. They became frustrated when authorities responded to the ambiguity with inaction.

Not Every Broken Windows Is Repaired: The Police Resist Community Demands

Community group members believed that, as an institution that spread the broken windows gospel, the LAPD should have targeted illegal vending. A senior lead officer and neighborhood prosecutor were assigned to the area specifically for the purpose of addressing local "quality-of-life" concerns on a long-term basis. In community meetings and in the press, LAPD officers constantly talked about their belief in broken windows. For example, at a community meeting an LAPD officer talked about the importance of quickly addressing graffiti: "When we see graffiti, we try to get it removed as soon as possible because the broken windows theory that we follow says that if we clean it off quickly people will be less tempted to put more graffiti on top of it. Our goal is for the gang to see that they cannot thrive here and move on to another area."

The mediation of enforcement through reporting technology exemplified the push and pull between police and community groups over their relative power in partnerships. The COMPSTAT system (short for complaint statistics) structured officer deployment and accountability in the broken windows model of policing (Bratton and Malinowski 2008; Parenti 2001). The COMPSTAT system mapped up-to-date crime trends with higher-crime areas getting more police. Commissioners and chiefs ranked LAPD divisions at monthly COMPSTAT meetings according to the percentage that captains brought down crime in their reporting districts.

Police often advised residents to report vendors. Community group members were told that the more they could document disorder, the more resources would be distributed to the area. It was a recurring tactic of appeasement that officers could fall back on when other responses proved insufficient.

Community group members were conscious of the COMPSTAT system and the broken windows theory. They actively tried to make their areas look like they were in dire need of police resources. According to one community group member,

> People need to report everything. They see a lot, but they don't report it because they think nothing will happen. But when people make reports, it goes into COMPSTAT, and COMPSTAT determines officer deployment. So when no one reports, and officers look to COMPSTAT to decide where to send officers, they look at the map, and say, "Well, you live in a country club, there's no crime there."

But the process was not so straightforward. Although the point of broken windows is to focus on minor, not even technically illegal, offenses as a preventative measure, the daily reality of police work often necessitated deviation from this model. Vending was a low priority compared to robberies or assaults. Thus, a dedicated response was unlikely even if residents reported vendors consistently. From the perspective of the police, community group members overstepped their role. Police, not residents, decided enforcement.

The broken windows model granted officers broad discretion. An officer did not target *every* disorderly behavior. Rather, broken windows logic meant they could rely on a litany of charges of disorder to justify targeting the person or group at hand. For example, in a study of the LAPD, Steve Herbert (1997) discovered that police were reluctant to arrest street vendors as long as they did not challenge the police for territorial control. Nonetheless, police could not always brush off community groups based on the privilege of discretion. They still had to give at least a nod to the guidelines of community policing. Officers also justified their nonenforcement of vending ordinances by contesting community group members' definition of insiders and outsiders. For example, after years of unsuccessful demands for the citation and arrest of vendors, the LACH Community Group called for the assignment of a new senior lead officer. The senior lead officer under fire responded to the anger of LACH Community Group members in a letter, saying,

> This is also a social problem that politicians and government has been trying to solve for years. As a side note when other officers and myself attempt to cite these individuals we have been yelled at and ridiculed by citizens who claim that we are harassing and racial profiling these vendors. There is support for these vendors by people who say that this is a victimless crime and who claim that these vendors are merely serving a community who wants, needs and welcomes their services.

The senior lead officer pointed out that a sizable proportion of residents who were not involved in community groups showed approval of vendors by keeping them in business. When police enlisted residents in community partnerships they opened up a floodgate for which they were not prepared. Because "every moment of discomfort can be read as a potential broken window and therefore the first step on the road to chaos," residents bombarded police officers with a myriad of complaints (Chesluk 2004, 255).

Like the officers in William Lyons's (1999) study of a community partnership in Seattle, officers did not automatically imbue more educated, wealthy, and active community members with the authority to represent the community. Officers constructed a broader definition of community, at least momentarily, when community groups overstepped their role. Officers were flexible in their loyalty to broken windows logic depending upon the practical situations they faced. Nonetheless, the self-appointed community was determined to not be so easily dismissed.

COMMUNITY GROUPS TAKE ACTION: EMPOWERMENT AS VICTIMS AND CONSUMERS

In the summer of 2008 a white homeowner expressed his frustration with the persistence of illegal vending on his block:

> I do not care if the renters in the owner-neglected apartments want the vendors here, many of which are illegal aliens and or leaching

off of the welfare system or taking advantage of Section 8. I have already witnessed a surge in foot vendors this summer alone, some of which in broken English have told me they just got here from El Salvador. What's the chance they are here legally, operating a legal business? How is it that renters and illegal vendors have more rights in this neighborhood than the law-abiding, hard working tax-paying home-owning citizens? (La Cienega Heights Community Group 2008)

His statement is a common example of the way homeowners in the community groups talked about vendors and the patrons of vendors. The group that they considered to have a legitimate voice in the neighborhood was quite narrow. In their calls for action from authorities, the members of community groups revealed how they imagined themselves in relationship to other residents as well as to local government. To these ends, residents in community groups blended the frames of consumerism and victimization. They viewed local government not as a general public service but as an entity that must respond to an exclusive group of investors. The most obvious ground for entitlement was through the payment of property taxes. Community group members also made less concrete claims to entitlement. Because of their status as deserving urban citizenry (white or honorary white, "productive," not poor), they saw themselves and their property as constantly victimized by bad people. Community partnerships provided an avenue for residents to voice their demands and ideas about community within broken windows logic.

The security of self, property, and lifestyle was demanded as an entitlement of inclusion in the good, deserving community. Lisa Duggan (2003) argues that homeowners create exclusion through identification with the place in which they pay property taxes. Under the "consumer citizenship" model of government, they claim to be entitled to local government services in return for their investment (Duggan 2003, 38). The claim to exclusive services is far from purely economic. Rather, the localities to which homeowners identify are racial. High taxes are linked to "the high cost of welfare for poor, minority, urban residents—the same communities blamed for crime" (Simon 2007, 109). Community group members' claims for entitlement were saturated with racially coded implications about who is and who is not deserving of support from the state. "Illegal aliens," "broken English," "just got here from El Salvador," "leaching off of the welfare system or taking advantage of Section 8," "fatherless children" (stated by the same man) signal that the people being talked about were poor, black or brown, undeserving, and criminal. The victim is someone who pays while others are free riders.

Besides envisioning themselves as deserving of services because of taxes or long-term neighborhood involvement, residents in partnerships appealed to crime victimization. Scholars have noted that a victimization frame is often strategically successful in gaining legal footing (Glassner 1999; Garland 2001; Harcourt 2001; Simon 2007). Jonathan Simon (2007, 89–90) argues that with the 1968 Omnibus Crime Control and Safe Streets Act the crime victim arose as an "idealized subject." Legislation centered on the imagined interests of the victim. The exaltation of the victim as model citizen created incentives for people to embrace the identity. Therefore "people deploy the category of crime to legitimate interventions that have other motivations" (Simon 2007, 4). The process of defining dangerous others entailed the simultaneous definition of the self as potential victim.

Although community groups were dominated by property owners, the few renters in the groups also claimed to be invested in the neighborhood and entitled to services and a police response. In a regression of marginalization, longtime renters distanced themselves from people they considered unworthy and criminal, such as new renters or undocumented immigrants. For example, one of the few renters active in the LACH Community Group, a black woman, referred to working renters as the apartment dwellers deserving of a place in the community: "What I mean when I say working renters is that these were not transient renters. Many had been in the neighborhood for 20 years." Renters leveraged the time or energy they invested and their status as good people to elicit a response from police, local government, and city prosecutors. Community group members believed that they got nothing back for all their hard work and material investment, not even extensive special treatment from local bureaucracies. Meanwhile, undeserving and lazy others lived charmed lives blessed with protection by the state.

Empowerment through Politicking

Whereas most of the members of the LACH Community Group had little sway with police and neighborhood prosecutors, members of the Community–Police Advisory Board (C-PAB) often maintained daily communication with the WLAPD captain and negotiated their concerns with him or her directly. The advisory board members were mainly white homeowners from affluent Westside neighborhoods.

David, a white business owner on the board of C-PAB, was active in his neighborhood council and a member of the chamber of commerce. David had little tolerance for residents who insisted that police were the answer to community problems. He told me that the community had to be empowered to solve its own problems, "We have a responsibility to take matters into our own hands. We can't wait for the cops or the city to solve this. It is a matter of personal responsibility." At a neighborhood watch meeting for La Cienega Heights, David explained how his neighborhood association successfully solicited city services:

> City government is like a big tree. And I can be an arborist but you guys have to learn how to work the system. My suggestion is that if you want something to get done submit a request in writing, e-mail is fine, to your city council person. And report it to your neighborhood council. The neighborhood council advises the city council on quality-of-life issues. And don't forget about it. Keep calling and checking up on it. . . . you have to know who to go to but also how to talk to them.

The WLAPD captain confirmed the soundness of David's advice: "David is right about persistence. If someone calls me once, obviously I look at it. But if someone calls me 15 times, guess what? The person who calls me once is going on the backburner."

David played a role in a lawsuit which blocked the Pico-Olympic Traffic Initiative proposed by Mayor Antonio Villaraigosa and then City Councilmember Jack Weiss. The purpose of the initiative was to alleviate a portion of Los Angeles's notorious traffic problems by changing the parallel Pico Boulevard and Olympic Boulevard into one-way streets during rush hours. The neighborhood councils along Pico felt they were left out of the decision process when the initiative was crafted. Furthermore, businesses were convinced they would lose revenue from the extensive parking restrictions that would accompany the change in traffic signals. With donations from Westside homeowners, the chamber of commerce hired a lawyer and successfully defeated the initiative.

David used the leverage he gained from the Pico-Olympic Traffic Initiative lawsuit to facilitate antivending enforcement. At a public safety meeting, the WLAPD captain, with David at his side, explained to a crowd of angry residents why it is not practically feasible for the police to confiscate vendor's goods.

CAPTAIN: We don't have space for confiscated goods. That would require a warehouse and the problem is that property in West LA is expensive. The pushcarts are technically evidence in a crime. But we are working on—

DAVID (CUTTING IN): C-PAB is currently working on getting space. Along Pico there are some owners of public storage places who are very grateful to us for stopping the Pico-Olympic traffic initiative.

The purpose of C-PAB was to provide a liaison between the community and the police. Advisory board members were supposed to represent the concerns of the community. Alternately, C-PAB members assisted the LAPD in community policing efforts such as Neighborhood Watch. Police-appointed liaisons in community-police partnerships structured community expectations of police (Crawford 1997; Garland 2001; Chesluk 2004). Thus the groups legitimated LAPD actions as backed by popular support and a democratic process. In a way, David was trying to help the WLAPD captain by providing him with resources to which he would not otherwise have access and appease demanding residents. It is common in community partnerships for police to develop their own agenda and then "tap community partnerships only insofar as they are a resource for the police department, reversing the power flow from empowering communities to empowering the police" (Lyons 1999, 36).

Powerful and wealthy civilians can use their resources to support police. For example, several residents in the police-community partnership were also part of the Los Angeles Police Foundation, which provides private financial support to the LAPD. When the West LAPD had their ammunition budget reduced by the city, the Police Foundation swooped in to replace the funds.

Nevertheless, appointing civilians who possess power, wealth, or influence can bring tension to a partnership. They can leverage their resources to persuade police to respond to their needs and forcefully challenge claims of responsibility and blame made by officials. Although the police had state authority, some community group members were much wealthier and, in many ways, more politically connected than the police captains with whom they partnered. David's unique position also brought subtle tension to police power. The sincerity of the captain's desire to address vending was checked when community group members viably offered solutions. Interestingly, however, such power differentials may backfire. During the course of this research, David was ousted from C-PAB. The newly appointed captain made use of her right to remove any C-PAB member. When other C-PAB members demanded transparency over the circumstances of David's removal, she would only comment that they had a "difference of opinion." She replaced David with a "more respectful" soft-spoken white man in his sixties from Bel-Air. At least in the arena of C-PAB, it appears the police held onto ultimate authority. Most community group members, however, did not have the resources to battle the WLAPD captain. They had a more immediate and direct method to confront vending.

Empowerment through Vigilantism

The neighborhood prosecutor explained in an interview why she believed that vending was such a salient issue for community group members: "People don't like strangers in their neighborhood. So it's perceived that if you have this person sitting there selling fruit, somehow these people are doing something else—some other illegal activity."

Community group members insisted that vendors had no place in the neighborhood. But the vendors were not strangers in the sense that they were unfamiliar to residents. There was a general consistency day after day in the people who drove the produce trucks, sold ice cream from pushcarts, and set up fruit stands at busy corners. Patrons developed amicable acquaintanceships with the vendors they regularly bought from. The police also knew the vendors who frequented the neighborhood.

Community group members who opposed vending recognized particular vendors. One LACH Community Group member burst out of his house to yell at a vendor he claimed was arrogant for repeatedly ignoring requests to stop honking his horn. In another instance, a member of the group was arrested after a vendor called the police to report harassment. Community group members harbored vehement anger at the vendors they believed filed false battery claims against them. When community group members could not elicit a response from authorities, they took enforcement into their own hands. A LACH Community Group member started a 2008 letter with the line "Word from the front" as if to imply the existence of a war between some residents and vendors. He continued, "If something dramatic is not done soon with regard to shutting down these vendors, escalation of confrontation is inevitable" (La Cienega Heights Community Group 2008). Community group members positioned themselves as under siege from a litany of undeserving, criminal people and from the very institutions that were supposed to protect them. They simultaneously defined community narrowly while employing populist language to justify taking action into their own hands.

In order to get a response from the authorities, residents tracked vendors, called the police, and refused to leave until the police agreed to meet their demands for a citation or arrest. Another LACH Community Group member advanced a sort of ultimatum to the neighborhood prosecutor, "If this area is not policed, we will have to do it ourselves, at great personal risk." The community group member admitted to me that she personally struggled with the turn the community group took: "We have had to do citizens arrests. We have had to follow people we saw breaking into houses or doing graffiti and hold them until the police get there. At what point does it turn into vigilantism? We don't want to do that." There was uncertainty and unease in all parts of the partnership as to when the "informal regulation of criminal deviance" slipped from neighborly vigilance into uncontrollable vigilantism (Johnston 1996, 220). What are the police to do when the residents who are supposed to restore order become themselves disorderly? For the core members of community partnership groups, crime prevention became all-encompassing. They maintained constant communication with police, city prosecutors, and government officials, checked COMPSTAT crime maps daily, and discussed any signs of possible danger with each other via call chains. Look for deviance through a broken window and you will see it, sometimes driving a produce truck.

THE DISORDER OF UPSTANDING CITIZENS

Community and broken windows policing presume very different legitimate roles for community members. Yet both policing approaches are not incompatible and may be used to the advantage of community members. Once a community buys into the premise of broken windows they may relinquish their presumed passive role and try to hold the police accountable to the causal link between disorder and crime. Community group members turned the tables, demanding protective services in the name of looming disorder. How much did community group members, a small but vocal portion of the neighborhood population, actually associate vendors with crime and danger? Community group members themselves may not even have been certain as to why they felt as they did about vendors. It is difficult to disentangle true motivations from instrumental tactics. It is evident, however, that community group members used harm arguments selectively and strategically to prompt a desired response from authorities. When their harm arguments were rejected, community group members turned to making more direct connections between vending and danger, for example, through claims that vendors dealt drugs and burglarized homes.

Community group members explicitly stated that they were using the broken windows framework and that they expected the police to do the same. For years, community groups were told by police that it was important to follow the broken windows model by erasing graffiti immediately, fixing broken street lights, and keeping up their lawns and houses. Residents, however, turned expectations back on the police. They were comfortable engaging with academic theories. They understood how COMPSTAT and officer deployment worked enough to actively manipulate police technology. Using the broken windows framework heightened the level of attention residents expected from police and other local government agencies. The community's warm embrace of broken windows surveillance put the police in the awkward position of having to qualify the causal links between street vending and serious crime. A policy that was supposed to give law enforcement discretion to single out disorder was used to encourage them to spend scarce resources. It was community group members that sought preventative action on the assumption, however tenuous, that the worst situation would materialize.

In taking a risk management framework, community groups overestimated the likelihood of danger, especially in a neighborhood where murders and violent crime were relatively rare. Although the stated intent of community partnership programs was to reduce fear, the broken windows theory allowed community group members to argue that potential danger was everywhere.

Battles over vending in the racially and socioeconomically mixed area highlight that, contrary to the claims of broken windows advocates, what constitutes disorder is far from obvious. Order does not magically arise out of disorder. Rather, constructing order produces the problem of disorder. Moreover, what is order in one context becomes disorderly in another context (Berg and Timmermans 2000, 47). Here, harnessing the broken windows argument in the framework of community policing gave community groups leverage to define street vending as disorder. Community groups became quite chaotic in their own way as they scrambled from one line of logic to another. In the end, community group members never got the dedicated systematic enforcement they wanted. The tentacles of formal and informal social control functioned unevenly and uneasily. It involved a variety of actors who often worked at cross-purposes.

Community group members saw broken windows logic as offering a promised land of order that was worth almost any cost. But their frantic need to tame disorder haphazardly affected the daily lives of vendors and other groups they criminalized. Moreover, there was a lifelessness that permeated the spaces where there loomed fear of anything that winked openly of the uncomfortable or of indecency or wild beauty. In many cities unsanctioned art is attacked as criminal graffiti (Ferrell 1995, 79). Skateboarding is categorized as a public nuisance (Hayward 2004, 142). The community group was like many urban entities that continue to arrange and regulate public space in their own binary vision, erasing any complexity. Street vendors selling food were feared as door-to-door deliverymen of chaos and crime. The ordering obsession suffocated any traces of creativity and excitement. The utopia of controlled space, the numbing need for civility and blank walls, is no place to end up.

Community-police partnerships in the 2000s were the starting point from which I followed a thread back to the 1950s. I traced the trajectory of Cadillac-Corning from a neighborhood dominated by white, middle class residents in single-family homes through a sudden demographic change to an African American, and later Latino, working-class neighborhood. By the 1960s, Cadillac-Corning was viewed by outsiders as a violent enclave. Housing development and school desegregation set a path for the policy and practice of stigmatization and militarization. The creation and implementation of Los Angeles City's first gang injunction exacerbated suppression into the 1980s. In current times, the neighborhood is a site for the tense negotiation of broken windows and community policing.

While tracing this process, I have been haunted by a passage by Milan Kundera, words that have laced themselves through my brain have not stop tugging:

> We have more and more universities and more and more students. If students are going to earn degrees, they've got to come up with dissertation topics. And since dissertations can be written about everything under the sun, the number of topics is infinite. Sheets of paper covered with words pile up in archives sadder than cemeteries, because no one ever visits them, not even on All Soul's Day. Culture is perishing in overproduction, in an avalanche of words, in the madness of quantity. . . . He resigned himself to a sea of words with no weight and no resemblance to life. (1999, 103)

My world is bursting with words. I love words. Just as I find the sacred in desert land, I find the sacred in words. But I need to give them weight. I need them to be alive. When I looked at all the pieces of my research together, I saw a partial map of city and county power. I had gained insight into how the City Attorney's Office, privileged community groups, the LAPD, and business groups cooperated and conflicted as they shaped Los Angeles. Moreover, I saw the momentum of history, a series of small decisions built up over time to make a neighborhood a target for suppression. Could this map be useful in efforts to dismantle the system of suppression and build alternatives to mass incarceration and surveillance? Could we take advantage of the points of tension between influential civilians and authorities to create schisms, upset policy, and interfere with practice? Could we use the historical case study as a guide to where we should look—at mundane, routine meetings in which important decisions are arrived at and acted upon? I honestly didn't know if the answer was yes to any of these questions, but I had an obsession with finding out.

Since I arrived in Los Angeles in 2007, I had been part of a group called the Youth Justice Coalition. From the beginning, I found the people in the coalition irreverent and creative, attacking the system from all sides—using direct action, space liberation, policy development, meetings with officials, and public education, all driven by the youth and communities that were most affected by violence and suppression. The next chapter documents an attempt to perform lively and artistic research on gang injunctions in a way that reframes the public safety debate. We employed the research on power in Los Angeles in the preceding chapters to our strategic advantage as we challenged the criminalization of youth.

CHAPTER 5

"We Don't Need No Gang Injunction! We Just Out Here Tryin' to Function!"

IT HAPPENS SO FAST and it feels inescapable. Silver Lake was the hotspot but then, just as quickly, it was over. Onto Echo Park, Highland Park, it never ends. The secret is out—cheap rents, charming old houses to flip. All that needs to be done is to clean out some of the people that have been hanging around the area for generations. The lady that sells papusas gets to stay. The new crowd likes papusas. Beware: gentrification and displacement are tearing through neighborhoods.

On June 18, 2013, Dennis Romero with the LA Weekly published a blog post entitled, "Can Echo Park Hipsters Be Safe from Gangs?" The post discussed the outgoing LA City Attorney Carmen Trutanich's plans for the proposed Glendale Corridor Gang Injunction targeting the Big Top Locos, Crazys, Diamond Street Locos, Echo Park Locos, Frogtown, and Head Hunters (Romero 2013). Although the injunction covered several neighborhoods, including Silver Lake and Elysian Park (home to Dodger Stadium), it became known casually as the "Echo Park Gang Injunction."

Why an injunction in the Echo Park area? Why now? It was not because of crime or community demand. Some things, however, have changed greatly in Echo Park and nearby areas over the last couple of decades. They are the same things that changed in Cadillac-Corning before the 1987 injunction—race and development. All the players I laid out in the previous chapters of the book—police, city prosecutors, neighborhood councils, business owners—came into play very clearly with the Glendale Corridor Gang Injunction.

This chapter's title comes from a Youth Justice Coalition (YJC) chant and documents my experience as a researcher and organizer with that group. Some of the research throughout this book was also used by other Youth Justice Coalition members to create popular education tools, which can be viewed at the Youth Justice Coalition website (www.youth4justice .org). The words in this book are my take on the gang injunction struggle, focusing on the power brokers attempting to pass the injunction. Therefore, the chapter is in no way a comprehensive overview of all the people and groups involved in the struggle. Furthermore, I do not address some aspects of the Glendale Corridor Gang Injunction struggle because I do not want to reveal ongoing organizing and legal strategies.

INJUNCTIONS, GENTRIFICATION, AND DISPLACEMENT

Since 1987, the Los Angeles City Attorney's Office has quietly implemented over 45 gang injunctions. At the time the majority of these injunctions were approved, most of the public had no idea what a gang injunction was. Where there was discussion about injunctions, the talk was generally supportive. For the small section of the public that was familiar with them, gang injunctions promised relief from street violence. Business owners favored gang injunctions because they legalized the removal of "undesirables" from middle-class entertainment and consumer centers (Boga 1993; Davis 2006). For politicians, supporting injunctions offered an easy way to appear tough on crime. Moreover, careers are made off of injunctions. For example a gang prosecutor contracted with an unincorporated city in Los Angeles County to write one injunction for $260,000. The funds were paid through asset forfeiture. Lastly, injunctions allow police to bypass due process and probable cause. Like nearly any employee, officers want to make their jobs as easy as possible and prime themselves for promotion. Unlike most employees, officers' attempts to make their job easier can decimate peoples' lives.

Injunctions originally were intended to remove people of color from public space by confining them to private residences. Over time, however, the injunction became a tool of displacement rather than confinement—a way to rid populations from target areas. In Glendale Corridor Gang Injunction declarations, an officer states that the alleged gang

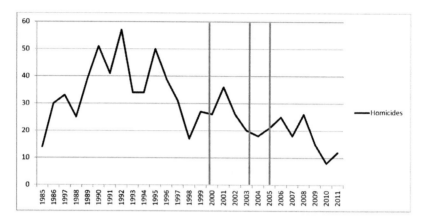

FIGURE 7 Los Angeles Police Department Northeast Division homicides by year (with previous gang injunctions marked). Source: Los Angeles Police Department (1985–2011).

members in Echo Park keep a low profile "staying hidden inside their homes" (*People v. Big Top Locos* 2013a). The stated purpose of an injunction is to keep people from associating with one another in public. The police acknowledge that this is already being done. So what is the purpose of the injunction if not to push people out of public view? To push people out of the neighborhood altogether.

A Los Angeles County police officer shared in an interview that he considered a previous injunction in his patrol area successful because it forced alleged gang members to move out of his reporting district and encouraged new businesses to move in. He exclaimed, "We've got Bed Bath and Beyond now! We've got Starbucks now! We've got In and Out Burger . . . here!" Some officers are aware that injunctions lead to gentrification and that gentrification can make being an officer easier.

However, moving violence around the county, the state, the nation, and the world is not public safety. Eventually, the roots of violence have to be addressed rather than pushed temporarily out of sight. The Glendale Corridor Gang Injunction was never about public safety. The two LAPD divisions—Rampart and Northeast—with jurisdiction over the proposed injunction area had the lowest crime rates in 30 years.

The drop in crime coincided with a demographic change. Young, affluent, mostly white people had moved into Echo Park and neighboring

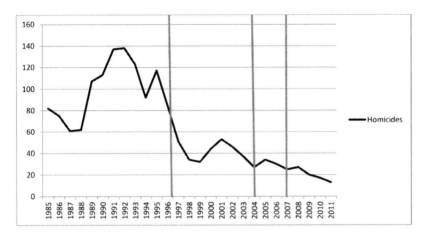

FIGURE 8 LAPD Rampart Division homicides by year (with previous gang injunctions marked). Source: Los Angeles Police Department (1985–2011).

Silver Lake en masse (see Table 1). It is a famous or infamous (depending on if you are the displaced or the displacer) center for West Coast hipsters. In court documents, a LAPD Gang Unit officer refers to new gentrifying residents as "urban pioneers" (*People v. Big Top Locos* 2013a).

In a court declaration, an officer recognized that downtown development had already pushed out many of the people targeted by the Glendale Corridor Gang Injunction: "With all the development of the Civic Center and Bunker Hill, there is really not much of Diamond Street left" (*People v. Big Top Locos* 2013b). Diamond Street is a neighborhood targeted by the Glendale Corridor Gang Injunction.

Another officer commented on attracting businesses to the Glendale Corridor area:

> There is a lot of commercial property along the river in the western edge of this area. If you were a business person, wanting a site for your company, and you looked at a for lease sign with gang graffiti including a reference to 13, meaning the prison gang, the Mexican Mafia, would you even get out of your car to look at the site? Or would you take your business and its jobs to a location where the signs do not have gang graffiti on them? (*People v. Big Top Locos* 2013c)

TABLE 1

Census Tracts in 10026 Area Code (Proposed Injunction Area)

Census Tract	% white (non-Latino), 1991	% white (non-Latino), 2007–2011	% change
1955	31.9	49.2	+17.3
1956	13.6	22.7	+9.1
1975	12.1	22.4	+10.3
1973	16.1	27.4	+11.3

SOURCE: U.S. Bureau of the Census (1990c, 2007–2011).

Since 1987, injunctions have continued to be placed on communities of color that threaten the boundaries of white, middle-class neighborhoods. Increasingly targeted are neighborhoods that hamper the development of entertainment centers, business districts, and gentrified housing. Where there is an injunction, redevelopment is often close behind. For example, in 1997, the Los Angeles City Attorney's Office filed for a gang injunction against 18th Street. The injunction covered the Pico-Union area of Los Angeles. Pico-Union was home to a predominantly working-class, Latino, first-generation immigrant community. Across the street, Los Angeles officials were scouting sites for a new stadium for the Clippers, Lakers, and Kings professional sports teams. Shortly after, in 1998, construction began on the new stadium, the Staples Center, at 11th and Figueroa, right next to the Pico-Union neighborhood and the Los Angeles Convention Center. At the time, the Staples Center was the most expensive arena ever built. It included 160 suites for high rollers that sold for between $197,500 and $300,000. The suites were intended primarily for corporate entertaining. Corporations, law firms, and film studios could use the game as a meeting venue for big-money business dealings. The arena also included a high-end restaurant and an exclusive stadium bar with wine cellars and cigars stocked in humidors, which required $10,500 per year in dues to patronize (Elliott 1999).

Tim Leiweke, president of the Staples Center, commented to the media about the arena that "this building is the beacon for many of the hopes and aspirations of the city as to the economic rejuvenation of our downtown area" (Simmers and Wharton 1999). The Staples Center construction was part of a larger plan to create an entertainment hub in downtown Los Angeles. Developers and the city planned to build upscale lofts, restaurants, theaters, hotels, nightclubs, clothing, and jewelry stores that would make downtown an adult playground for the wealthy. A part of the Business Improvement District plan that was created for the downtown area included private security that would be accountable to downtown executives and that would be authorized to throw people who are homeless out of the area.

The 18th Street Pico-Union injunction was suspended in September 1999 because three of the six LAPD gang unit officers that presented evidence in favor of the injunction were involved in the Rampart corruption scandal (O'Deane 2007). More than 70 officers associated with the anti-gang Community Resources Against Street Hoodlums (CRASH) Unit had engaged in police misconduct, which included planting false evidence, police brutality, narcotics dealing, evidence theft, bank robbery, and perjury. In 2002, these injunctions were refiled by the City Attorney's Office. Consequently, they remain in effect today.

In the plan for downtown, the city also stated its intent to extend redevelopment along the Figueroa Corridor south to the University of Southern California (USC; see Davis 2002, 162). In 2001, the board of the Metropolitan Transportation Authority voted to move forward on the extension of the Los Angeles County Metro Rail System along the Figueroa Corridor south of downtown (Shuit 2001). The project was approved despite objections about noise from low-income downtown and USC-adjacent residents. The "Expo Line" would allow commuters to travel easily between downtown and USC, the site of the Los Angeles Memorial Coliseum in Exposition Park. Phase I of the Expo Line construction, from downtown to Culver City, began in 2006.

As the Expo Line rolled past USC, so did development and an injunction. In 2007, the city attorney filed a gang injunction against the Rolling 40s, 46 Top Dollar Hustler Crips, and 46 Neighborhood Crips. The enjoined area passes along the Expo Line just south of the borders of Exposition Park and USC. The first Expo Line stations opened in

2012. Real estate development inevitably followed. In 2011, construction began on developer Geoffrey H. Palmer's upscale USC student housing, "The Lorenzo." Gated off from the rest of South Central Los Angeles, the Lorenzo offers four resort swimming pools, five rooftop sundecks, two indoor basketball courts, five libraries with computer labs and study rooms, and a three-story fitness center (www.thelorenzo.com).

Public housing sites have been a main target for injunctions as well. Hope VI is a federal program that provides funding to upgrade or demolish and rebuild distressed public housing. While the idea sounds good, there is a record of Hope VI projects displacing low-income residents. Los Angeles public housing has been the site of several Hope VI projects that were executed shortly after or during the implementation of a gang injunction. Gang injunctions make it easier for the Housing Authority of the City of Los Angeles (HACLA) to evict public housing tenants.

In the late 1990s, the Los Angeles City Planning Department proposed the demolition of the Dana Strand housing project in the harbor area. The city planned to "revitalize" the neighborhood through the replacement of Dana Strand housing with a "mixed-income community." In practice, a mixed-income community means that a number of low-income residents will be displaced because the new development does not have enough affordable units for current residents. A portion of the new units in mixed-income developments are market rate. Moreover, the new development can have fewer units than the original. The City Planning Department argued that Dana Strand was "desperately in need of redevelopment in order to arrest the spread of decline to the adjoining areas" (Los Angeles Department of City Planning 2001).

Dana Strand residents successfully stopped the first application for Hope VI funds that would be used to demolish their homes in 1999 (Williams 2003). The Housing Authority unsuccessfully applied a total of five times for a Hope VI revitalization grant. It was successful, however, in attaining a demolition grant in 2001. The same year, the Los Angeles City Attorney filed for a gang injunction within the boundaries of Dana Strand. In 2003, the old Dana Strand of 389 units was demolished and replaced with 116 townhomes (Mercy Housing 2012). The redevelopment of Dana Strand was a collaboration between nonprofit housing organizations Mercy Housing California and Abode

Communities, private developer ROEM Corporation, HACLA, and the Los Angeles Police Department.

Nickerson Gardens and Jordan Downs are other examples of redevelopment occurring shortly after injunctions. The Bounty Hunters injunction was implemented in Nickerson Gardens in 2003. The Los Angeles City Planning Department stated their intent to apply for Hope VI funds in 2001 and 2003 to "redevelop" Nickerson Gardens into a "mixed-income/use" area. After the 2005 Grape Street injunction, the city began planning the development of Jordan Downs public housing project into a "vibrant urban village that is sustainable, mixed-use, mixed-income" (Urban Land Institute 2009).

THE MODERN GANG INJUNCTION:
ALLEGATION, ASSOCIATION, AND DISCRETION

Three themes form the core of the modern-day gang injunction: the determination of gang membership, the association provision, and police discretion. The information for this section is drawn primarily from Glendale Corridor Gang Injunction legal documents and original research by the Youth Justice Coalition's REALsearch Center. Starting in 2012, the Youth Justice Coalition began conducting ongoing research on the impact of gang injunctions and gang databases on those most affected—people listed on injunctions, friends and family of enjoined people, and those who live and work in injunction areas in Los Angeles County. Establishing if someone was listed on an injunction was difficult and at times, not possible, which is why the research includes people affected by injunctions even if they are not officially enjoined. For example, some people had never been served with injunction paperwork but had been subject to an arrest where an officer has used the injunction as justification.

The impact of gang injunctions was assessed using a mixed methods approach that included interviews, short-form surveys, long-form surveys, GIS mapping, statistical analysis, and ethnographic observation. I use the research results to discuss the daily impacts of the determination of gang membership, the association provision, and police discretion. The juxtaposition of text and experience is to demonstrate how legal language functions as action in the street.

Determining Gang Membership

The following are symbols and brands that, if worn or included in a tattoo, may be considered in determining gang membership within the Glendale Corridor Gang Injunction zone (*People v. Big Top Locos* 2013):

- Diamond Supply Co. gear or a picture of a diamond
- Duke Blue Devils gear
- Aztec warrior symbols
- 90026 zip code
- Los Angeles Dodger's logo
- Rhino logo from Mark Ecko gear
- Mickey's Malt Liquor hornet
- Anything gear with the letter B, including but not limited to the Boston Bruins, Brooklyn Dodgers, and UCLA Bruins
- A frog (One of the more absurd pieces of evidence of membership in the Frogtown gang included a frog stuffed animal that police found when they searched someone's room)
- The color green
- The color blue
- Belt buckle with the letter E

A controversial aspect of injunctions is the determination of gang membership. As I have discussed throughout this book, authorities have a heavily flawed, racist, and assumption-packed process for determining gang membership. It is lacking in rigor and can be considered vague and inconsistent, at best. In Mara Dauber's (2014, 37–38) ethnographic examination of police in the Glendale Corridor Gang Injunction area, an officer argued that, although a given crime "may not fit the criteria for gangs, I could probably point, or draw the nexus between gangs and that crime, whatever it is."

A good portion of the Glendale Corridor Gang Injunction declarations are dedicated to establishing gang membership. An officer explained that when determining gang membership, "There are specific criteria we look for and document: self-admission, gang tattoos, gang clothing, being in a neighborhood, etc." (*People v. Big Top Locos* 2013c). The following two statements from LAPD officers, pulled from court declarations, illustrate the problematic and overly broad determination of gang membership:

Sometimes a person will admit his gang membership, not by what he says or what he does, but by what he chooses to wear that day. Echo Park gang members will wear Mark Ecko clothing. Good people in the neighborhood know that and would not wear Ecko clothing because they do not want anyone to think they are a gang member. (*People v. Big Top Locos* 2013a)

If I see a frog tattoo on someone in the Frogtown area, I will think that person very likely might be a Frogtown gang member. I will look for other clues, but it is hard to imagine someone getting a frog tattoo simply because they like frogs, especially in that neighborhood. . . . Even if someone likes frogs for whatever reason, if they are not a gang member, they would not wear a shirt or get a tattoo depicting frogs because they would know that frogs are a symbol used by the gang. (*People v. Big Top Locos* 2013c)

Here, the officers confuse "would not" with legally "cannot." Police and prosecutors have an opinion that a good person would not wear certain brands or have certain tattoos. But that should be different from it being illegal for a person to do so.

During the fight against the Glendale Corridor Gang Injunction, in November 2013, the U.S. Court of Appeals for the Ninth Circuit issued a ruling in the *Vasquez v. Rackacuckas* case. The Ninth Circuit found that the Orange County, California, District Attorney violated due process rights in a gang injunction against Orange Varrio Cypress. The court ruled that the Orange County District Attorney's Office did not have an adequate process to determine gang membership. Thus they put broad restrictions on enjoined people without first providing adequate evidence that they were gang members. The court ruled that enjoined people must be "afforded an adequate opportunity to contest whether they are active gang members before they are subjected to the injunction" (*Vasquez v. Rackacuckas* 2013). A postdeprivation removal process was not an adequate replacement because the burden was shifted to petitioners, rather than the state, to prove that they were not active gang members. As I explain later in the section, the Los Angeles Superior Court judge did not believe that the *Vasquez v. Rackacuckas* ruling was applicable to the Glendale Corridor Gang Injunction.

The flippant identification of a person as a gang member has psychological and material consequences. One participant in the Youth Justice Coalition research explained in an interview,

> Many youngsters have been chased out of the community and city. They have to be more alone and get by themselves because they are arrested with family or in groups. They have had to move away. I see a lot of people in my community harassed. Many police have personal issues, and they find loopholes and reasons to take out race hatred or personal frustrations on our community. People get violated or pulled over on their way to work and get there late, get in trouble or fired. Police mess with people that are not gang involved but they throw in the towel after so much harassment and say, "Well I might as well represent if I'm going to get treated like it." There have been numerous arrests since the injunction without convictions. People can't keep jobs. It doesn't look good to employers or professors when you have that kind of contact with the system.

In the Youth Justice Coalition research, 33% of respondents said that an injunction affected their ability to get a job, while 26% said that an injunction affected their ability to keep a job. For 23% of respondents, school attendance was affected by an injunction. For 24% of respondents, an injunction affected access to public housing/Section 8.

Association

The association provision is, and always has been, the heart of the gang injunction. The prosecutors who write the injunction language are willing to make many concessions in order to keep the association provision untouched. For example, the Glendale Corridor Gang Injunction contains a five-year "burn-off" provision in which the injunction is deemed enforceable against an individual within five years of being served with the injunction. After five years, authorities must serve the individual with new injunction papers for the order to be enforceable. The Glendale Corridor Gang Injunction service paperwork that an individual receives when they are put on the injunction also includes a "petition for removal." If enjoined persons do not believe they belong on the injunction, they can immediately file for removal. The removal process is problematic, of course, because enjoined persons request removal from the same people—the City Attorney's Office—who put them on the injunction in the first place. As I discuss in Chapter 3, the removal process takes months (during which the petitioners are still subject to the injunction) and requires that petitioners not have law enforcement *contact* (not arrest or conviction, but just simple contact) for two years prior.

Notably absent is a curfew provision, which until recently was a central component of every injunction. There is no curfew for enjoined people in current gang injunctions that are overseen by the LAPD, not because the injunction authors made the choice to exclude the provision, but due to a federal class action lawsuit. The 2011 lawsuit, filed by lead plaintiffs Alberto Cazarez and Christian Rodriguez, alleged that sundown curfews in gang injunction were unconstitutional. In response, LAPD command issued an order that officers were no longer authorized to enforce the curfew provision of 26 gang injunctions (Charles 2013). In the fall of 2013, the lawsuit was brought to the Ninth Circuit Court of Appeals on the claim that the Los Angeles City Attorney's Office was not making a good-faith effort to locate those affected by the order and inform them that the curfew provision was no longer enforceable. According to a 2014 California Public Records Act request, the Los Angeles City Attorney's Office does not even possess a list of currently enjoined people. A ruling on the case has not yet been issued.

All of these provisions, while positive steps, do not address the heart of the gang injunction—the association provision. It is the first point listed in the injunction and is extensively detailed:

a. Do not Associate: Standing, sitting, walking, driving, gathering, or appearing, anywhere in public view, in any public place, or any place accessible to the public, with any other known member of a Defendant Gang. This prohibition shall not apply in any of the following situations: (1) when an enjoined person is inside the premises of a licensed school attending class or conducting school business, or (2) when an enjoined person is inside the premises of a church or religious institution for purposes of worship, or (3) when an enjoined person is inside a place where he/she is lawfully employed and is engaged in a lawful business, trade, profession, or occupation which requires such presence. This prohibition against associating shall apply to methods of travel to and from any of the aforementioned permissible locations. For the purpose of this provision, and every provision where it is mentioned, public place is defined as any place to which the public has access, including but not to sidewalks, alleys, streets, highways, parks, hospitals, office buildings, transport facilities, businesses, and the common areas of schools;

b. Do Not Associate in Common Areas: Standing, sitting, walking, driving, gathering, or appearing, with any other known member of any Defendant Gang, in a common area, courtyard, or carport of any apartment complex, condominium, or townhome. (*People v. Big Top Locos* 2013)

Note that the exception for academic study, worship, and employment only applies when a person is inside a building. Alberto Cazarez, a Youth Justice Coalition organizer and lead plaintiff in the curfew lawsuit described above, is from the Mar Vista Gardens in the Culver City area of Los Angeles. He is listed on a gang injunction for standing with a neighbor. Alberto remembers police waiting outside of the doors to his school to ticket students who walked home together. His teacher had to escort students home in waves.

In interviews and surveys conducted by the Youth Justice Coalition, 49% of respondents said that an injunction restricted them from attending family gatherings. Forty-one percent responded that an injunction restricted them from attending community events. Because of the ease with which the gang member label is applied, it is common for entire families to become enjoined. People living with or hanging out with an alleged gang member come to be considered gang members or gang associates.

The gang injunction association provision makes mundane tasks a stressful, possibly jailable act. Twenty-two percent of respondents in the Youth Justice Coalition research said that an injunction affected their ability to go the grocery store. One respondent explained, "I asked my friend to take me to the store but we can't ride in the same car because we are both on an injunction. We can't have family gatherings or even Thanksgiving dinner because the police come and harass us." Another respondent stated, "Always getting pulled over and making me late to stuff. Everyone in the community gets pulled over. Every time I go to the store or pick my daughters from school, police harass me. It slows down my schedule." Twenty-two percent of people said that the injunction restricted them from visitation from their own children. Thirty percent of respondents said that an injunction affected their ability to attend a funeral.

Police Discretion

A primary reason the community affected by the Glendale Corridor Gang Injunction opposed the measure was the discretion that an injunction confers upon police. The LAPD is notorious for its unjustifiable "excessive use of force" against unarmed civilians, which is often a euphemism for assault or murder by a police officer.

Injunctions broaden officer discretion. Consequently, an officer can pull over Latino men with shaved heads and use the injunction to pick from a variety of justifications. Dauber (2014, 36) observed officers openly using the injunction as an after-the-fact justification to racially profile:

> When asked what the typical Gang Unit officer looks for when out on the streets, one officer replied without hesitation, "four Hispanic guys riding around with shaved heads . . . they could be gang members, they could be police cadets, you won't know until you pull them over and talk to them." . . . The officer continued, stating that what you would look for in another area of the city would be different, giving the example of Black men and "O.G. cars like Monte Carlos" in Southcentral.

The officer continued that they injunction is a great tool for the police because it "provides that legal reason to stop" (Dauber 2014, 41).

The consequences of increased police discretion range from unwarranted stops to fatalities. A study by University of Southern California graduate students uncovered that murders of unarmed civilians by police officers were higher in neighborhoods that had gang injunctions than in areas that were not covered by injunctions (Ellison and Lenz 2012). Authorities use accusations of gang membership to justify shootings of civilians.

As part of the Youth Justice Coalition research, participants were asked about trust between the police and the policed community as well as police violence against civilians (Table 2). Several points stand out in the responses to these five questions. For one, the most common answer to how violence in the neighborhood has been affected by an injunction was, "stayed the same." A majority of residents did not see a noticeable change in street violence after the implementation of an injunction. Forty-three percent of residents interviewed did see at least some increase, however, in the level of police violence against the community, consistent with Treva Ellison and Colby Lenz's (2012) results. In a possibly related result, 51% of respondents said that trust between the community and the police decreased a little or a lot. One person interviewed explained, "I am more cautious, less forthcoming with the police. I'm concerned about guarding my life. Now I try to hide when I hear them coming."

TABLE 2

Youth Justice Coalition Community Survey Results (in %)

Since the injunction . . .	Decreased a lot	Decreased a little	Stayed the same	Increased a little	Increased a lot
1. Violence in your neighborhood has:	3	12	41	9	13
2. Police presence has:	2	4	17	11	42
3. Trust between the community and police has:	41	10	17	7	2
4. Police violence against the community has:	3	7	25	17	26
5. Stops by the police have:	2	3	13	8	34

Note: Percentages do not sum to 100% because some participants declined to answer the question.

COMMUNITY RESISTANCE:
DETERMINED TO S.T.A.Y.

After the proposed injunction was announced, community members from targeted neighborhoods and their allies met to discuss the repercussions. Several of the meetings took place by the Echo Park Lake and at Chuco's Justice Center in Inglewood, California. Community members decided to oppose the injunction. A community group, Standing Together Advocating for our Youth (S.T.A.Y.) was formed under the motto, "United We Stand, Together We S.T.A.Y."

Immediately after the community began meeting, the National Association of Town Watch and LAPD planned to hold National Night Out events in various parts of the city. The National Association of Town Watch materials describe National Night Out as "an effort to promote involvement in crime prevention activities, police-community partnerships, neighborhood camaraderie and send a message to criminals letting them know that neighborhoods are organized and fighting back" (natw .org). Perhaps the neighborhood was too organized because in the midst of the injunction battle, the Echo Park Night Out was canceled. Community members resisted the injunction through multiple avenues, including appealing to and ultimately overtaking the neighborhood council, launching a legal challenge, community organizing, and Cop Watch, in which residents monitor and document police interaction with civilians.

Return of the Neighborhood Council

Fighting the Glendale Corridor Gang Injunction, I found myself back in that farcical democratic façade—the neighborhood council. Though I suppose they could be highjacked and used for the stated purposes of egalitarian citizen involvement in local government, and although there are exceptions, more often than not I have found neighborhood councils to be stacked with relatively conservative, powerful, and well-off people who support the police. The city tries to use neighborhood councils to justify its actions as community-based (see Chapter 4 as an example). For this reason, neighborhood councils are an important site of contention.

The proposed injunction area included the jurisdictions of the Silver Lake Neighborhood Council and the Greater Elysian Echo Park Neighborhood Council. On August 8, 2013, backed with community support,

three Silver Lake Neighborhood Council members presented a resolu-
tion to not support the Glendale Corridor Gang Injunction. In response,
the Silver Lake Neighborhood Council decided to hold a public safety
forum to discuss the proposed injunction. I accepted the request to speak
on a panel at the Silver Lake Public Safety Forum about the proposed
injunction. Besides me, the opposing side included a longtime resident of
Echo Park and S.T.A.Y. founder, Rio Jill Contreras, as well as an ACLU
staff attorney. Supporting the injunction were a member of another
neighborhood council, a representative from the City Attorney's Office,
and a Rampart Division officer. The police and prosecutors brought
along an extensive entourage of LAPD officers and multiple prosecutors
from the City Attorney's Office, including several people that I had previously interviewed for this research. The panel sat in front of the room.
The pack of authorities sat near the front on my right-hand side. The rest
of the room was full of the residents of neighborhoods covered by the
proposed injunction. It would become clear through the meeting that
nearly all of the residents present vehemently opposed the injunction.

Over the years of observing authorities, I've noticed a pattern in
the way they react to challenges. They reliably run through a variety of
tactics when opposed by community members. I always want to understand how power functions. Therefore, I describe here the narrative of
the meeting by breaking it into five chunks that analyze the responses
of authorities: dismissal, objective rationality, emotional manipulation,
benevolent imperialism, and appeasement.

1. DISMISSAL. For the first part of the panel, residents submitted question cards. Both the sides opposing and supporting the injunction would
then have two minutes each to give a response. In response to a question
as to why residents were not consulted about the injunction, the representative for the City Attorney's Office offered the following explanation:
"I do not have to consult with you before I bring a case. That is not my
job." Authorities began with a straightforward demonstration of power;
they would move ahead with cases without consulting with regular people simply because they could.

When asked subsequent questions about why they were continuing
with the injunction despite community objections, the City Attorney's
Office representative responded with a slightly altered dismissal: "You

represent a small group. We represent the community. We have talked to other groups. They feel very differently." Similarly, court declarations by police officers and gang prosecutors are filled with statements like "People have told me . . ." (*People v. Big Top Locos* 2013a). Like the example I presented in Chapter 4 of this book, the City Attorney's Office representative was trying to create a definition of community that served its position. Opposition brought by community members was dismissed by referring to a vague entity of "other supportive community members." When pressed as to who these people were, authorities responded that they could not reveal identities without placing injunction supporters in danger.

2. OBJECTIVE RATIONALITY. It is difficult for authority to spend an entire two-hour meeting practicing dismissal. It is not impossible. I have seen it done, but it is difficult. Often they must fall back on other tactics. At this point in the challenge, authority is usually still relatively calm and secure. Police and prosecutors start to rely on statistics, often times with no citations. Crime is up, so we need more suppression-based policing. Or crime is down, which proves that suppression-based policing works. Either way, the answer is more cops, more drones, more guns, more jail cells. The trouble with debating authorities is that they can lie without consequence.

For example, I was interviewed on a Southern California public radio station about the Glendale Corridor Gang Injunction. The counterpoints to my position were represented by an LAPD captain and a neighborhood council president. I pointed out that there were no long-term studies proving the effectiveness of gang injunctions as a long-term public safety strategy. The LAPD captain argued that there were studies. He could not, however, cite any. Although he promised to get the studies to the host of the radio show and to me at a later time, he never did. The same thing occurred in the Silver Lake panel. The same thing happens regularly in public interactions with authority. It does not matter that the captain never presents those studies because they do not exist. Listeners of that radio program are given the impression that they might.

The same was true for the public safety forum. The Rampart Division officer on the panel acknowledged that crime was decreasing. He argued, however, that "gang-related" crime still made up a large proportion of the existing crime rates. Sometimes he said that about 30% of crime in the area was gang related. Other times the percentage he threw out was 25% or 15%. Who knows? Certainly the police and city prosecutors did not. What is important is that statistics tend to intimidate or mesmerize people. Invented or not, percentages give legitimacy to authorities' claims.

Dauber (2014, 23) also observed that the LAPD and the LA City Attorney's Office claim that gang injunctions have "a clearly demonstrable positive affect [*sic*] on the neighborhood area covered," and even a "remarkable effect." Dauber also mentions that the LAPD and LA City Attorney's Office fail to substantiate their claims in any way.

3. EMOTIONAL MANIPULATION. When statistics fail to silence opposition, authority pulls out anecdotes about murders, often involving children. At one point, the Rampart Division officer on the panel held up a sheet of paper, announcing that it was a story from the *Los Angeles Times* about the murder of a toddler in a drive-by shooting. It was later discovered that the murder to which he referred happened four years prior to the introduction of the gang injunction. The obvious purpose of this tactic is to incite fear. The cops were saying, "You need us to protect you. If you do not listen to us, if this gang injunction is not passed, it could be your child next."

Another purpose is, again, legitimacy. The officer continued, "I know certain groups in this community do not have extensive contacts with the gangs like other people do. You do not have to see what we have to see as officers. I've seen a four-year-old shot and killed after she was caught in the cross fire of a drive by." This appeal to fear and pain, however, is only effective against detached advocacy organizations in which employees are from a world different from the one clients represent. Long-term residents of the area and grassroots groups in which the people most affected advocate for themselves experience violence all the time. Chances are the four-year-old whose death is being used as political currency is one of our children. The police cannot claim the moral high ground.

4. BENEVOLENT IMPERIALISM. There is a new, disturbing justification for gang injunctions. At public forums, officers and prosecutors

consistently claimed that the injunction is in the interests of alleged gang members listed on the injunction. They argued that people would be safer on the injunction because if they are not outside in public, then they will not be shot. The authors of the injunction claim that gang injunctions are good for defendants because, if people are locked out of sight, they cannot be hurt.

In court declarations, an officer from the Echo Park area claimed that a gang injunction is for the good of youth that live under the rule of the LAPD because the injunction will keep them "from continuing in their fathers' gangster footsteps" (*People v. Big Top Locos* 2013a). Again, there is no evidence that an injunction will do so. In fact, there is evidence to the contrary, that injunctions lock people into dependence on illegal activities by blocking marginalized communities from resources in favor of over policing and incarceration.

The same officer's declaration continued,

> Sometimes Echo Park gang members will rob people on Sunset, although perhaps not as much as one might expect. I think the gangsters know that the newer visitors and residents will call the police. Echo Park and other gang members tend to prey on more vulnerable people, like undocumented workers, who they believe are less likely to report being a victim or witness of crime to the police (*People v. Big Top Locos* 2013a).

Police and prosecutors argued that the injunction would be beneficial to vulnerable people while they simultaneously criminalized immigrant street vendors and day laborers. Furthermore, as stated above, gang injunctions appear to increase civilian fear of police, potentially making crime reports less likely, particularly by undocumented people.

5. APPEASEMENT. When community members hold their position, as was the case in this meeting, and do not buy the dismissal, the statistics, the horror stories, and the patronizing logic as a justification for what power wants to do, authority turns to appeasement. They try to play nice so that they can de-escalate the challenge. Often this means making people feel like they are respected and that their input will be taken seriously.

It became apparent during the public safety forum that the City Attorney's Office intended to go through with the injunction regardless of what resulted from any meeting with community members. By the end of the forum, authorities tried to tempter the momentum of the opposition through appeasement. The following statements were made by city prosecutors:

> "We will take your opinion under consideration. We are going to take what we have heard today back and discuss it with the City Attorney."

> "We represent you."

> "Isn't this dialogue great? This is a democratic process!"

The Rampart Division officer also tried to close the meeting on a more friendly note, stating, "We want the same thing—safety. We work with the community in the same way that you do."

There are the prosecutors of the world for whom the legal system is quite clear: there are good guys and bad guys. They are squarely on the side of justice. Justice looks like kicking ass in court. If they think someone looks like a bad guy, wears what the bad guys wear, lives where the bad guys live, they should be punished without mercy. For these prosecutors, leniency and bleeding hearts are what is wrong with the world.

But there are others, too. For example, one of the city prosecutors present at the public safety forum began a career representing residents who were fighting for better housing conditions against slumlords. She identified her experience fighting for housing rights as a main motivation to become a prosecutor. I got the feeling she did not want to be at the panel. It seemed like she was not thoroughly behind the injunction. She was quiet nearly the entire time. At the end of the meeting she stood up and, almost pleadingly, said that the City Attorney's Office did not want to be in conflict with the community: "When I go into court I represent you. You are the People of the State of California on whose behalf we will be bringing the injunction against the gangs." The response was groans and laughter from the crowd. The prosecutor sat down and stared at the papers on her lap.

A few minutes later, during public comment, a community member unequivocally rejected the prosecutor's statement that she represented the community. This prosecutor looked stunned. Knowing her past as I did, I tried to imagine what it must be like to hear that. How does one come so far from what they wanted to be? Does it happen slowly, over time, tiny changes that go unnoticed? I also wondered what it must be like to have your desk next to one of the self-proclaimed good guys.

A couple of weeks after the public safety forum, the Silver Lake Neighborhood Council convened to vote on a motion to not support the Glendale Corridor Gang Injunction. The other neighborhood council within the proposed gang injunction zone, the Greater Echo Park Elysian Neighborhood Council, had just voted unanimously to oppose the injunction. Several Greater Echo Park Elysian Neighborhood Council members decided to oppose the injunction after youth living in injunction neighborhoods spoke at the meeting about the devastating impact of injunctions on their lives.

More than 100 people showed up to the Silver Lake Neighborhood Council meeting to speak about the Glendale Corridor Gang Injunction. The neighborhood council president announced that no public comment would be allowed. Residents immediately objected and started public comment at the microphone anyway. After much scurrying, the neighborhood council adjourned for 15 minutes.

Upon returning, the neighborhood council president announced that public comments would be allowed, at 30 seconds per comment. Fourteen of the 21 neighborhood council members were present. Before the vote, the neighborhood council president recused herself from voting. After public comment, eight council members voted to not support the injunction. Seven members voted to support the injunction. At that point, the neighborhood council president reversed her initial commitment to abstain from voting. She voted to support the injunction, creating a tie. An additional member of the neighborhood council suddenly appeared and stated his intention to vote. The parliamentarian in charge of the meeting rules told the councilmember that he could not vote because he was absent from public comments. After some whispering between the parliamentarian and the neighborhood council, it was announced that the newly arrived councilmember would be allowed to

FIGURE 9 The Silver Lake Neighborhood Council meeting to vote on the Glendale Corridor Gang Injunction. Youth organizer Mario Rodriguez takes charge of public comment after Silver Lake Neighborhood Council members (in the background) refuse to allow the public to speak about the Glendale Corridor Gang Injunction. Photo by Adam Vine.

vote. He voted in favor of the injunction. The final vote ended up as nine in support of the injunction, eight in opposition.

The outraged crowd began shouting, "We don't need no gang injunction, we're just out here trying to function!" Because of the chanting, the council was unable to move on to the rest of the agenda items. The meeting was adjourned, and a dozen LAPD officers, including the Northeast Division captain, were called in for backup. The officers immediately declared an illegal assembly. The crowd dispersed. The Northeast Division captain handed his card out to several people saying he would love to speak to the community more about injunctions. He admitted that although most of the community was against the injunction, they would pursue it anyway.

Los Angeles City neighborhood councils held elections in April 2014. Members and supporters of S.T.A.Y. took the majority of seats on the Silver Lake and Echo Park neighborhood councils. The former proinjunction president of the Echo Park Neighborhood Council was ousted in favor of S.T.A.Y.'s Kwazi Nkrumah. This year should be interesting.

FIGURE 10 The Silver Lake Neighborhood Council meeting to vote on the Glendale Corridor Gang Injunction. The Northeast Division of the Los Angeles Police Department arrives. Organizer Kim McGill speaks in the foreground. Photo by Adam Vine.

Direct Action

In September 2013 community members met with the incoming city attorney, Mike Feuer, to discuss their concerns with the proposed injunction. Feuer and his staff made clear that they would move forward with the injunction regardless of community input. In response, the Youth Justice Coalition, S.T.A.Y., members of the Echo Park and Silver Lake neighborhood councils, students, community residents, and community organizations of the Echo Park, Silver Lake, Elysian Valley, Temple-Beaudry, and Frog Town communities gathered outside of his downtown office during the first week of October. The purpose of the gathering was to serve three people: City Attorney Mike Feuer and two assistant city attorneys with a community injunction.

The community injunction, authored by Kim McGill and the Youth Justice Coalition, enjoined the three attorneys for failing to meet with the community before implementing a gang injunction, failing to protect the rights of low-income people and communities of color, and prioritizing the interests of private developers in Northeast Los Angeles. The three attorneys were ordered to avoid associating with other attorneys, judges, real estate developers, chamber of commerce members, business improvement district representatives, law enforcement officers, and neighborhood council representatives. The city attorney was also ordered to not accept campaign contributions from the above entities. The order further imposed an evening curfew, restricted the three attorneys from being within 500 feet of a courthouse, accepting subcontracts from other cities to write injunctions, or engaging in suppression-oriented policies. The order reserved the right to add up to 300 John Doe's to the injunction at any time.

The punishment for violation of the community injunction included being forced to spend a week in juvenile hall, county jail, or on the streets with a young person of color to experience the constant harassment, surveillance, and dehumanization of life under gang injunction. Continued violation of the order would result in removal from city employment and property confiscation (Youth Justice Coalition 2014).

Another anti-injunction action occurred around Halloween. In 2007, a video went viral of prisoners in the Philippines performing to Michael Jackson's pop song "Thriller." In the video, orange jumpsuit–clad men inside a maximum security detention facility act out the choreographed dance portrayed in the "Thriller" video, with the song booming in the background. To bring attention to the gang injunction, Youth Justice Coalition organizers decided to stage a similar performance at a busy intersection in Echo Park.

At about 6:00 P.M., dozens of cyclists surrounded all four sides of the intersection of Sunset Boulevard and Echo Park Avenue. The group was part of the S.T.A.Y. community bike ride against injunctions, the Bike Ride for Freedom. Attached to their bikes were signs proclaiming, "Injunction Equals Injustice," "Stop/Pare the Gang Injunction," and "Stop the Attacks on Brown and Black Youth." A van pulled into the intersection. The back doors swung open and the first beats of Thriller poured out. Fifteen or so people, most of them youth organizers, bounced into the intersection. Their faces were piled with globs of green and gray, which dripped onto their black flak jackets. All the dancers had "POLICE" printed across their black shirts in bright white letters. For a few minutes, traffic in Echo Park was immobilized by a group of youth dressed as zombie cops.

FIGURE 11 Anti–gang injunction action: "Zombie Takeover" activist flyer, designed by Kim McGill.

It took about two minutes for a police chopper to swoop in. An omniscient static voice commanded the dancers to disperse. In the video of Michael Jackson's "Thriller," zombies attack a young woman on a date. In this version of "Thriller," zombie cops attempted to attack a young person suspected of being a gang member. In the final moments of the performance, as the young person fought off the officers of the living dead, the chopper got its response: the mocking laughter that closes out the song.

Legal Challenge

On August 21, 2013, Over 250 community members turned out to oppose the Glendale Corridor Gang Injunction at the civil court hearing. A press conference and protest were held outside the courthouse. A contingent of about 50 residents packed the courtroom during the hearing.

FIGURE 12 Youth Organizer Jose Gallegos at the anti–gang injunction "Zombie Takeover. Photo by author.

Despite earlier reassurance from a LA City Attorney's Office representative that the community would be able to speak at the hearing, no one but attorneys were allowed to comment. The ruling was delayed.

The Youth Justice Coalition called together a legal team to challenge the injunction, which included pro bono attorneys, organizers, and residents of neighborhoods targeted by the Glendale Corridor Gang Injunction. Upon receipt of declarations and depositions from the police requesting the injunction, YJC researchers mapped out the locations and people referred to in the documents and systematically fact-checked all the claims.

FIGURE 13 Anti-injunction organizers protest the Glendale Corridor Gang Injunction in front of the Los Angeles Superior Court Building. Photo by Adam Vine.

The legal team got word on September 26, 2013, that the judge had granted the Glendale Corridor Gang Injunction. The ruling, though unfortunate, however, was not an ending but a beginning. When the City Attorney's Office files for a preliminary gang injunction, most of the time no one responds. I have seen a judge laugh with the city prosecutor over the fact that no one named in the declarations showed up to defend themselves. There is no legal pathway to respond to a gang injunction, especially in the case of a gang-only injunction. With gang-only injunctions, prosecutors do not initially serve individuals. Although individuals may be named in officers' declarations, the court order enjoins the gang as a whole. For example, in the Glendale Corridor Injunction, the defendants are listed as, "BIG TOP LOCOS AKA BIG TOP AKA BTLS AS CRAZYS AKA CYS AKA MAYBERRY AS DIAMOND STREET LOCOS AKA LOCOS AS ECHO PARK LOCOS AS FROGTOWN RIFA AS HEAD HUNTERS" (*People v. Big Top Locos* 2013). In order to respond, an attorney has to claim to represent the so-called gang. If an individual does respond, they would essentially be incriminating themselves as a shot caller in the gang.

When no one responds, which is often the case, the prosecutor files for a default judgment. In the Glendale Corridor case, the prosecutor filed for a default judgment on September 6, 2013. The judgment to grant the injunction was issued on September 24, 2013. The speed at which defaults are granted depends upon the particular judge's calendar. A default judgment, however, typically takes months. The granting of Glendale Corridor Gang Injunction was a surprise because it took two weeks instead of several months. Why the default judgment moved so quickly is unknown. But anti-injunction organizers could not help but wonder if it was pushed through out of political interest.

Gang injunctions usually meander slowly through the courts under the radar. When they are challenged legally, it is after they have been implemented. Attorneys sue after the injunction has been in place for some time and after people had already been arrested under the injunction. This strategy is usually unsuccessful. It is difficult to repeal injunctions. Even if an injunction is retroactively repealed, people have already had to live under the martial law that comes with an injunction and spent time in jail/prison because of the injunction. The catch-22 is that in order to legally oppose the injunction, an attorney has to represent the gang. Therefore, people have to incriminate themselves as fitting the state definition of a gang.

In the Glendale Corridor Gang Injunction case, the legal team found a way around this through the use of community interveners. There are two types of interveners. One is a person who has been named in the depositions as an alleged gang member. But as an intervener, that person is not admitting to gang membership. Rather, the intervener is claiming that, if the injunction were to pass, he or she very likely would be directly affected—that is, enjoined. Since police have named that person in declarations as a person they will target under the injunction, that person should have a legal right to oppose the proposed injunction at a court hearing. The second type of intervener is a person who is not likely to be directly affected. That person, however, lives in the neighborhoods targeted in the injunction. Consequently, that person's neighborhood and overall quality of life will be affected by the injunction. Several of the interveners in the second category were members of the Silver Lake Neighborhood Council and Greater Echo Park Elysian Neighborhood Council. They argued that, as elected officials, they should have been consulted before an injunction was introduced.

The first set of interveners had a hearing that took place on November 13, 2013. The hearing was brief and hostile. The *Vasquez* decision (see above) occurred the day before the attorney's briefs were due. Therefore, the briefs did not contain arguments about *Vasquez*. The Judge refused to consider the *Vasquez* decision.

The second set of interveners received a hearing on January 31, 2014. But there was not supposed to be a second hearing. The presiding judge initially denied all motions to intervene—those that were heard at the November 13 hearing as well as those who had not yet been heard. The judge reasoned that the postdeprivation process (the application to be removed from the injunction) was adequate. The judge also argued that the interveners could intervene only after they were served. Later, the judge set an additional court date for January 31 to hear the second set of proposed interveners. He claimed that the initial denial of all interveners was due to a clerical error.

The legal team brought a court recorder to the hearing for the second round of interveners. Transcripts of intervener hearings would be important in the case of an appeal. Because of budget cuts, Los Angeles Superior courtrooms do not automatically have court recorders. Plaintiffs or defendants must hire their own. The attorney for the interveners was able to argue that the *Vasquez* ruling was relevant to the Glendale Corridor Gang Injunction. At one point in the hearing, the city prosecutor claimed that the Greater Echo Park Elysian Neighborhood Council vote to not support the injunction was invalid because "gang members" were posted at the doors of neighborhood council meetings. Counsel for the interveners responded that it was exactly these type of careless and overbroad accusations of gang membership that warranted a hearing.

On February 3, 2014, the court released a ruling that denied all motions to intervene, stating that the *Vasquez* case was not relevant. The court ruled that people were not able to intervene if they were not served. The City Attorney's Office, however, at that point was not serving individuals as part of the Glendale Corridor Gang Injunction. The legal challenge will continue on appeal.

Community Resisters Targeted

Shortly after opposing the injunction, several Echo Park, Silver Lake, and Elysian Park community members were slapped with various charges. A Greater Echo Park Elysian Neighborhood Council member who introduced the motion against the injunction was accused by the Los Angeles City Attorney's Office of "riot making" for organizing a nonviolent march. After the community rallied behind him and several other defendants, the charges were dropped.

After the controversial Silver Lake Neighborhood Council vote on the injunction motion, the Silver Lake Neighborhood Council members in favor of the injunction brought a motion against the audience and the neighborhood council members opposed to the injunction. The motion accused the anti-injunction neighborhood council members of inciting violence in a government setting. The motion was eventually tabled.

As the injunction fight wore on, Echo Park residents noticed an increase in low-flying choppers, stop-and-frisks of youth, and police raids in their neighborhood. In April 2014, LAPD officers raided the homes of several Echo Park anti-injunction organizers on the claim that they were investigating involvement in a murder that occurred over four years prior. The resulting case is ongoing.

CONCLUSION: NEXT STEPS

From the beginning of the fight against the Glendale Corridor Gang Injunction, research was utilized by both sides. When the injunction was first announced, the Youth Justice Coalition's REALsearch Center compiled a fact sheet on gang injunctions and their connection to crime rates, racial change, patterns of gentrification, and private development across the city and in the proposed injunction area specifically. Additionally, the Youth Justice Coalition released occasional results from the ongoing research on the impact of gang injunctions and gang databases. Organizers used the results to debate the purpose, effectiveness, and continued use of the injunction. Research results emerged in neighborhood council meetings, in legal arguments, in the media, and at public education events. Gang injunction advocates responded with their own research.

During the writing of this chapter, the Los Angeles City Attorney's Office began handing out their own survey at neighborhood council events. The survey was entitled "Glendale Blvd Corridor Public Safety

Project Community Survey." Considering the current political climate, the survey was a thinly veiled attempt by the City Attorney's Office to collect data supporting their contention that the area covered by the Glendale Corridor Gang Injunction was plagued by gang and drug activity and, therefore, in desperate need of injunctive relief.

The Glendale Blvd Corridor Public Safety Project Community Survey is a poor data collection instrument. It is not possible to answer the survey in an objective way. The answers are skewed to lead the respondent to answer that drug and gang activity is a problem. The Glendale Blvd Corridor Public Safety Project Community Survey has glaring design flaws, including leading questions, double-barreled questions, the potential for inflated frequency rates, irrelevant comparisons and measurements, and lack of adequate response options. I have yet to see how they make use of the research results.

The police and prosecutors faced organized community opposition, several legal challenges, and unusually defiant neighborhood councils. Unlike in many other instances, the Echo Park and Silver Lake neighborhood councils refused to act as a community-based puppet for the LAPD and Los Angeles City Attorney's Office. I was curious to see what authorities would do next. What would they hold up as evidence of community support for their policies now that the neighborhood councils and other community groups were not cooperating? Ultimately, they moved ahead anyway, forgoing any façade of community support.

This chapter tracks what occurred after the Los Angeles City Attorney's Office announced the proposed gang injunction. Therefore it does not include the decades of work beforehand that people spent opposing injunctions on the street and in court. A couple of years ago, most people in Los Angeles had no idea what a gang injunction was. Today, gang injunctions are a much more common topic in news media. The public is talking about gang injunctions. And they are talking about them in the context of gentrification. The texture of the injunction-gentrification discourse happening now is the result of organizers saying these things over and over again for years until policy makers, popular media, and the general public finally began to reflect the language back. During the span of this timeline, organizers spoke about the Glendale Corridor Gang Injunction and injunctions generally at every possible venue. This timeline is in no way comprehensive.

Rarely, if ever, has a proposed gang injunction in LA incited the controversy and opposition that the Glendale Corridor Gang Injunction has. I believe there are several reasons for this. First, usually the public is not notified of an injunction until after it is implemented. Because of early coverage of the Glendale Corridor Gang Injunction, people had time to organize. Second, the Glendale Corridor Gang Injunction was blatantly a tactic of gentrification. Although gentrification, displacement, and development have been the driving force behind injunctions since their inception, it was undeniably clear in the Echo Park/Silver Lake areas, perhaps more so than in other injunctions. Third, greater numbers of high-profile, well-resourced people cared what happened in Echo Park than they did in Jordan Downs or Nickerson Gardens, for example. *Los Angeles Times* columnists, big-name attorneys, professors, and surgeons live in Echo Park and Silver Lake.

None of this diminishes the amazing efforts of all the organizers in the fight against the Glendale Corridor Gang Injunction and all injunctions. The political and social climate that proved conducive to a challenge was built by people who have been challenging gang injunctions and making the connection with gentrification for decades. The status of the Glendale Corridor Gang Injunction is still an open question. Consequently, I cannot give a perfectly packaged conclusion in the traditional sense.

The legal team has decided to appeal the Glendale Corridor Gang Injunction ruling to higher courts. The YJC will also continue releasing action research, including a report tentatively entitled "Land Grab," which will extensively document the relationship between injunctions, private development, gentrification, and displacement. Community organizers will continue to disrupt the courts, the police, and city officials through mass actions.

With the ousting of Mayor Antonio Villaraigosa and the election of Mayor Eric Garcetti, new members have been appointed to the Los Angeles Police Commission. The Police Commission is the official oversight body of the LAPD. The Police Commission, however, does little to no active oversight despite their investigative and veto power. One of the new appointees to the Police Commission is the executive director of El Centro del Pueblo, a community center in Echo Park. She publicly opposed the injunction.

FIGURE 14 Youth Organizer Tanisha Denard at anti–gang injunction action. Photo by Adam Vine.

It is also important to introduce nuanced discussion into the injunction debate. Authorities are hooked on the simple distinction between "good people" and "bad people" in the neighborhood. The legitimacy of the injunction relies on this infantile logic. No complex problem can be solved by starkly chopping the world into two simple categories. Great injustice inevitably occurs whenever those in power do so.

CHAPTER 6

Conclusion

I HAVE EXAMINED HOW police, city prosecutors, wealthy residents, and business owners in Los Angeles identify and target "dangerous" people. Community partnerships are the vehicle through which I chose to focus on current policing. I traced a genealogy of repression-oriented policies and practices in Los Angeles City through the development of multiple-unit housing in the 1940s, through school and residential desegregation in the 1960s, and through the city's first gang injunction in the 1980s.

What does all this tell us about power? Although I do not care what people in power think about us, I care a great deal about what they do. The ultimate end to this research was to understand and impede mechanisms of social domination. Several themes emerge from the research that illuminate the workings of official authority and competing modes of power.

THE CULTURAL EFFECT OF BROKEN
WINDOWS, COMMUNITY POLICING,
AND THE BRATTON LEGACY

Monday, July 15, 2013, was the day before Assata Shakur's birthday. I was working on the last chapters of this book when the LAPD called off a city-wide tactical alert that had been in effect since early the previous evening. It was sunrise, but I had slept little. People throughout the city protested the innocent verdict for George Zimmerman, the Florida neighborhood watch volunteer who murdered a 17-year-old African American man wearing a hoodie, Trayvon Martin. Martin was carrying Skittles candy and iced tea back from a convenience store when Zimmerman, claiming he was a threat, followed Martin, then shot and killed him. People across the nation held gatherings the weekend of July 13 and 14, 2013, after Zimmerman was found innocent by the jury and awarded his gun back. In Los Angeles, a group of people shut down a major vein of the city, the Interstate 10 Freeway.

Like so many people, I was angry despite expecting the innocent verdict. The outcome of the trial would not have changed the fact that a murder had occurred. But somehow none of that made it any less infuriating. It was one more confirmation that America functions under the framework of white supremacy and sanctioned anti-black violence. Two days before the Zimmerman verdict, there was a forum for the family of a 22-year-old man, D'Angelo Lopez, who was shot in the back and killed by a Los Angeles County sheriff. It seems to happen every week yet never makes the mainstream news. I am tired because there is just never a break in between funerals.

It did not surprise me that a neighborhood watch volunteer would murder an unarmed black youth. I spent years observing neighborhood watch volunteers whip themselves up over any person of color in a public space. I saw people who wore suits to work every day become enraptured by the idea of themselves as defenders of a frontier of respectability. City policies both sparked and reinforced profiling. As I mentioned in the previous chapter, an officer stated in his injunction declaration, "Sometimes a person will admit his gang membership, not by what he says or what he does, but by what he chose to wear that day" (*People v. Big Top Locos* 2013a). Police put this sentiment into action through racist stops and brutality. Some residents, emboldened by the principle, take to armed vigilantism. How many cities have community groups that look similar?

The effect of the broken windows framework on police interaction with the public, especially targeted groups, is attracting the attention of researchers. Equally intriguing and deserving of attention is the cultural effect of broken windows ideology on the general public. Chapter 4 of this book provides a peek into the effects broken windows ideology has on members of community groups on Los Angeles' Westside. I would be interested in comparative work based in other locations.

In Los Angeles, "community policing" seems to be eclipsing "broken windows" as the catchphrase of the moment. I argue throughout this book that there is considerable tension in LAPD attempts to carry out community policing. Traditional policing tactics and priorities still direct police resources. The department, however, has to at least appear to utilize community input. Often, officers try to tap into the resources of citizens in community groups for the benefit of the department. Nonetheless, wealthy and politically savvy residents in community groups can challenge this flow of power.

During William Bratton's tenure as police chief, a national myth arose—that community policing could improve police department relationships with communities of color. The LAPD portrays community policing in this light. But the actual relationship between LA cops and people of color is a subject that warrants an additional book. I will just say here that it is not the ideal partnership portrayed by the LAPD. It is a rather abusive marriage. Under Bratton, the LAPD did improve something—their public relations department. Under the community policing structure, they are obligated to listen to citizen requests. Afterward, they can walk out of the meeting, dump those requests into the trash, and continue as they intended to before the meeting. But has the substance of police work changed? I argue no. Yes, police officers and elected officials are willing to meet—but do not make the mistake of thinking it makes them allies.

In my study, community-police partnerships were closely related to neighborhood councils. There was overlap in the membership of community police advisory boards and neighborhood councils, especially the public safety committees. Since the inception of the neighborhood council system, police and city prosecutors have used neighborhood council support to claim that city policies are community based. In the Glendale Corridor Gang Injunction case, however, the neighborhood councils did not behave as they were supposed to. Residents and Greater Echo Park Elysian Neighborhood Council members introduced a motion proposing that the neighborhood council both oppose the injunction and build viable alternatives to the policing and incarceration of youth. The neighborhood council approved the motion unanimously. As I delineated in the previous chapter, the Silver Lake Neighborhood Council's vote was close and contested. The police and the City Attorney's Office attended meetings. They heard a lot of opposition. They moved through various strategies to manage the opposition (see Chapter 5, section "Return of the Neighborhood Council"). Then they moved forward with the injunction, anyway.

GANG INJUNCTIONS, THREATENED
SPACES, AND GENTRIFICATION

Scholars argue that the purpose of the modern criminal justice system is not to control crime but, rather, to control deviant groups, including racially deviant bodies (Alexander 2012). Using a color-blind risk management framework, people can hold positions that support racial inequality while sounding pragmatic (Bonilla-Silva 2001). The gang injunction is one of many purportedly race-neutral policies that target people of color. The development of gang injunctions is the elaboration of a dual system of criminal justice in which low-income urban people of color are targeted and given harsh punishment for things that are considered innocuous outside of stigmatized neighborhoods and the criminalized status of gang membership. Gang injunctions are reflective of a legal system designed to maintain racial boundaries without explicit mention of race.

The issue of when injunctions are put in place is an interesting one. Many injunctions seem to confirm and exacerbate processes already in progress. Gentrification and private development have started. The injunction is a way to displace the last of the unwanted residents, to pave the way for higher-end business development, and to reassure homebuyers. Other injunctions appear anecdotally tied to an attempt to spark gentrification. The injunction in South Central LA's Jordan Downs, for example, is not in an area that appears to be undergoing the extensive gentrification that marks Echo Park. City plans to tear the housing projects down and replace them with a mixed-income "urban village," however, will displace many current residents in favor or higher-income people. There needs to be further systematic examination of the factors that determine where and when injunctions are implemented—when gentrification is already in progress or to initiate gentrification.

The policies I examined, including gang injunctions, were first implemented in racially threatened spaces. Policies of force and control were instituted where the threat to the status quo was greatest. Borders separating black and white, wealthy and working class, were becoming porous. The Los Angeles School Board first banned transfers at Hamilton High School and two nearby middle schools because they were located in the corridor between the wealthy white part of the city and the rest of LA. At the time, Hamilton High School was undergoing white panic at rapid black integration in the neighborhood and schools. The desegregation-era militarization of the high school spilled over into the militarization of the local neighborhood, and vice versa. Moreover, the gang injunction was not implemented in the area with the most assaults or murders. The gang injunction was instituted where a drug business began negatively affecting white, middle- and upper-class people. The identification of Cadillac-Corning as the LAPD West Division's "worst area" was intentional. Some of the choicest real estate in the country is right across the street. Cadillac-Corning was and, in many ways, still is an abrupt dividing line in which authorities attempt to contain people of color.

During my research, one homeowner in a community group exclaimed, "This isn't Bel-Air. No one around here is just a kid!" Cadillac-Corning is not Bel-Air. The police retorted, however, that it is not South Central or East Los Angeles, the height of stigmatized territory in LA, either. The shoring up of threatened lines developed Cadillac-Corning as a sort of borderland space. Borderlands are places of untamed and destabilizing ambiguity. They are geopolitical spaces in flux. There is a lot at stake, which is why community groups, police, and policy makers dedicate so much time and resources to those spaces. They tried to turn upheaval into stasis and reestablish smudged lines.

TARGETING STATUS AND CREATING CRIMINALIZED CLASSES

Prosecutors and police argue that gang injunctions are needed to combat assaults, murders, burglaries, robberies, property crimes, drug use, and drug dealing. However, a penal code already exists to prosecute all of these crimes. Gang injunctions provide a legal justification for stop-and-frisk. They also provide enhanced sentencing that locks people up for longer or pushes them into pleas. Additional research is called for on the effect of stacking gang enhancements in order to get defendants to plea out rather than opt for a more costly jury trial.

The state marks alleged gang membership as the defining aspect of a person. According to this rubric, it is not one part of who they are as a human. It *is* who they are. Consequently, they can be dehumanized to the point that discrimination, brutality, torture, and even death.

One argument in favor of the injunction is that it creates a stigma that deters enjoined individuals from gang membership. Stigma, however, only works as a deterrent (if it ever works at all) when it is an exceptional event. Stigma and shaming are not effective when nearly everyone in a neighborhood is subjected to the stigmatized identity (Nagin 1999). If anything, the identity becomes normalized and a point of shared pride.

William J. Stuntz (2011) argues that American law no longer functions in the service of justice; rather, it is convenient for the keepers of law. (Stuntz and I diverge in that I would argue that it has never functioned in the service of justice.) As evidence, Stuntz points to the rampant tactic of charging people, rather than acts. Police and prosecutors have a myriad of justifications to choose from in order to arrest and incarcerate someone. For example, if an immigrant is accused of terrorism but a terrorism conviction is difficult to attain, authorities may charge that person with an immigration violation and deport him or her. It is common to charge alleged gang members on drug crimes, and vice versa. The result is that people are not convicted because of an action. Instead, authorities target a person and use whichever charges are more effective to convict them.

Strategies for Challenges

Sometimes power looks like a group of people sitting around a table and plotting. Unfortunately, not always. I say it is unfortunate because, if power always looked like that, it would be easier to defeat. The process of building policies, categories, and militarized practices is not always a simple top-down affair.

Change comes from unexpected places. When I stepped into the city archives to examine the roots of apartment building in Cadillac-Corning, I expected to find that development companies and city planners from outside the neighborhood were responsible for the transition from single-family homes. Most of the original multiple-unit development, however, was initiated by homeowners within Cadillac-Corning desiring additional income. Homeowners advocated on both sides of the issue with city government as the ultimate gatekeeper of development. Simultaneously, school desegregation policies allowed black families to enter Westside schools. Those families found Cadillac-Corning to be an accessible neighborhood in which to settle. The amalgamation of zone and set-back line changes by individual homeowners and small developers combined with the policy of school desegregation to result in racial turnover. The racist policies and practices that increased the militarization of Hamilton High School and Cadillac-Corning ended up stigmatizing the neighborhood. In a cycle, the stigmatization of the neighborhood resulted in a greater police presence that led to further stigmatization and the continuation of repressive policies.

In the tug of war between the police and residents in community partnerships, I was surprised to see more conservative militancy in community groups than within the police department. Community groups in West LA were antiegalitarian. They bypassed the state at times and took on the punishment of "deviant" groups through various levels of vigilantism. Community groups turned community policing on its head, making demands on the police more than they aided officers. The police and "community" conflicted in the way they defined disorder and the preferred method of addressing those deemed disorderly. The interplay among residents, business groups, homeowners associations, police, and government shaped the neighborhood. The frameworks used by police, such as broken windows, affected citizen expectations. As community groups pushed back on police, they, in turn, manipulated authority's use of frameworks. There was a tension between different types of power—influence, wealth, force, and authority. While police had a monopoly on authoritative force, wealthy residents had political connections and resources that even the police did not.

The word "community" conjures up warm, fuzzy romanticized images of people knowing, helping, and caring for one another (Crawford 1997; Lyons 1999). But "community" is a widely used and vague term. There are many kinds of communities, as defined by various people and constituency groups. The definition of "community" can also be a means for creating and reproducing inequality. In Cadillac-Corning, community groups became the official institutional spokespeople for the neighborhood because of their wealth, education, visibility, and political connections.

One lesson for organizers is the emergence of unlikely allies. The agencies of government and community groups often work at cross purposes, opening up pockets of weakness. The most effective way to launch challenges is to be up to date on the political context so that short-lived vulnerabilities that arise during power struggles can be exploited. Organizers must respond promptly to the unexpected and often unsystematic nature of force and control.

Furthermore, accidents of history have lasting effects. There was no Big Brother system that planned and instituted control in the cases that I probed. The target of LA City's first gang injunction was not meticulously picked by city attorneys and the LAPD from a map of the city that broke down crime rates. Rather, some prosecutors had an idea—and they happened to be stationed in the West LA Division. Of course, within West LA, the selection of Cadillac-Corning as the pilot neighborhood was intentional and racially driven. A precedent was set in which gang injunctions could be used to maintain racial borders. Moreover, the legacy of the injunction is still imprinted on the reputation of and policing tactics in Cadillac-Corning 20 years later. The practice of building gates at the end of alleyways to preclude getaway routes is still standard. Police continue to target youth on bicycles as suspected lookouts for the drug business. Similarly, the binders that police and city prosecutors used to document alleged gang members evolved into an ever-expanding gang database that sweeps thousands of youth into the system. The messy daily micropolitics of decision making added up to a matrix of repressive policies and practices (Staples 2000).

Although there was no ultimate master plan, the rise of certain people to positions of influence and the deployment of control and force were far from arbitrary. Contingency is everywhere. There is always the possibility that unexpected actors and situations arise that change the path of history. The path taken, however, is directional in important ways. Certain people are able to capitalize on the chances presented. As with the validation of community, people with material and social resources make arguments and take advantage of contingency. The majority of the working-class black and Latino residents did not have the resources to become the community in the "community partnership." Instead, a privileged minority was able to take advantage of the opportunity to declare themselves community spokespeople. They then urged and, at times, attempted to force police and city government to take repressive action against the majority of residents, with far-reaching consequences.

Political struggles are easily forgotten. The contentious process of creating categories and institutionalizing protocol often disappear, leaving only the categorization systems, protocols, and repeated practices. Azar Nafisi (2003, 22) captures the phenomenon perfectly when she states, "It is only through these empty rituals that brutality becomes possible." People carry out institutional ritual that, while seemingly benign, commits violence. Critical junctures occur when a choice is made to address a problem (Mahoney 2001). An institutional response is then created to deal with the problem. Initially, practices are often instituted because of a combination of accident and influence by well-resourced, capitalizing people. In their policy behavior, future actors within this institution are likely to follow the path set at the critical juncture. As authorities pull from available tools at hand, there are incentives to some decisions while others are restricted. People within institutions are socialized into the values of the institution (Gains, John, and Stoker 2005; Levin-Waldman 2009). Often, these values are inscribed as protocol, so they seem more like good common sense than subjective values. Once instituted, infrastructure takes on a life of its own. The intentions of original actors matter little once a practice is put into place.

The creation of the gang injunction, for example, is a critical juncture. Returning to the testimony for the Cadillac-Corning gang injunction exposes how police and city attorneys explicitly targeted black youth who were deemed threatening to surrounding white, middle-class areas. All the policies I address have racially disproportionate effects, yet authorities claim they are race neutral. For example, although the wording of gang injunction policies are sanitized of race, the testimony that informed Cadillac-Corning's injunction specifically targeted black youth as violent offenders from deviant families. Injecting historical memory and physical context back into those processes reveals what has been abstracted out. In policies regarding housing, schools, gang repression, and broken windows policing, there is a simultaneous sanitization of race and racially disproportionate effects. Policies like gang injunctions and broken windows policing, although they do not explicitly call for racially disproportionate treatment, result in negative outcomes for people of color. The policies were created to do so, and they are successful in that respect.

Furthermore, there is no final category or practice. Casually used categorization requires constant upkeep. With street vendors, community group members' arguments were not sufficient. Community groups had to constantly demonstrate to police that vendors were the disorderly deviants and they, the orderly law-abiders.

Research in and of itself is not the answer. Data will not bring liberation. Ultimately, I want people to oppose LA's treatment of youth because they feel it viscerally and ethically, because the knowledge enters them and becomes entwined in their insides—not because investigating murders of youth or locking them up is getting too costly.

Intimately understanding power dynamics in Los Angeles has been a fascinating and, at times, painful ride, both professionally and personally. Using that understanding to challenge repression-oriented policies has been incredible. As for the people in power, I am not saying we changed their minds and hearts. I would guess that very few changed their position in the end. They fell back on other research that supported their beliefs. Or, if none was available, they claimed that our work was somehow invalid. Evidence is always political.

Nonetheless, the challenge was important. Power hides behind statistics, graphs, and footnotes. When people unexpectedly have the logic they rely upon undermined, the reactions are interesting. Sometimes authority can be momentarily silenced. At other times, their true feelings come out. For small pockets of time, the people we challenged revealed what they actually thought. To the general public we provided an alternative claim to what the city government and police were saying. By questioning their position with well-done research, we undermined their complete authority a little.

With the battle over the Glendale Corridor Gang Injunction, gang injunctions as an issue gained more attention. Mainstream media followed the legal battle. The incoming city attorney, police commissioners, city prosecutors, and other politicians were asked their position on injunctions. The narrative that was constructed about the injunction was not one of crime and safety. The police and city officials were not able to roll out their common claim that gang injunctions are about protecting people. Their talking points were delegitimized early on by competing narratives. Most of the time, when injunctions were talked about in forums or covered in the media, it was connected to gentrification.

Some in positions of authority and the general public continued to deny the connection between gentrification and injunctions. Others, however, cracked. There were spaces where honest discussion was had. There were times people showed their hand and revealed who they really were. People admitted that the issue was gentrification, and, moreover, they thought gentrification was a good thing. For example, a local public radio station dedicated a show to debating the Glendale Corridor Gang Injunction. The show ran audio clips of interviews with people walking around Echo Park one weekend. The interviewer asked whether they were in support of or opposed to the injunction. One woman responded that she had mixed feelings about it because she herself was a recent "gentrifier" of Echo Park. She understood the damage caused by injunctions. Ultimately, however, she stated that she would support the injunction because it was it was in the interests of her and her children.

I do not believe it is worthwhile to conduct research that focuses solely on the harm done to marginalized people. I have never seen change result from people telling their stories of struggle to people in power. Pity does not force the hand of authority. People of color are often expected to give away stories to outsiders. But analysis is where the power is. We already know that poverty is rampant. We know police brutality is scarring and killing people of color. We know mass incarceration is hurting us. But I want to know how oppression happens. Show me *how*. Then maybe I will know how to disrupt it in the most effective ways.

I believe, at its best, this is what research can do—not provide a disguise of rationalizations for those in power to hide behind. Instead it can crack the mask open and reveal all the vulnerability, passion, hate, beauty, and ugliness. Maybe that will get us somewhere if we are able to expose the play of power more often. But maybe I am too cynical. Maybe when we uncover the people behind the power, we will find that their masks and their flesh have not become permanently sutured together.

References

ACLU Foundation of Southern California. 1997. "False Premise/False Promise: The Blythe Street Gang Injunction and Its Aftermath." Los Angeles: American Civil Liberties Union Foundation of Southern California. https://www.acluso-cal.org/issues/police-practices/false-premise-false-promise-blythe-street-gang-injunction.

Alexander, Michelle. 2012. *The New Jim Crow: Mass Incarceration in the Age of Color-blindness.* New York: New Press.

Allan, Edward L. 2004. *Civil Gang Abatement: The Effectiveness and Implications of Policing by Injunction.* New York: LFB Scholarly Publishing.

Alonzo, Alex. 1999. "Territoriality among African-American Street Gangs in Los Angeles." Master's thesis, Department of Geography, University of Southern California.

Baird, Barbara. 1980. "Burke Opposes Temescal School Site." *Los Angeles Times,* January 31, WS2.

Barajas, Frank. 2007. "An Invading Army: A Civil Gang Injunction in a Southern California Chicana/o Community." *Latino Studies* 5:393–417.

Baum, Mr. Macy, and Mrs. Macy Baum. 1963. "Letter to Los Angeles City Clerk Walter C. Patterson." n.d. Council File No. 114090, City Planning Case nos. 11497 and 14744. Los Angeles: Los Angeles City Archives.

Becker, Howard. 1997. *Outsiders: Studies in the Sociology of Deviance.* New York: Free Press.

Berg, Marc, and Stefan Timmermans. 2000. "Orders and Their Others: On the Constitution of Universalities in Medical Work." Configurations 8 (1): 31–61.

Bickel, Christopher. 2012. "From Black Codes to Gang Injunctions: Apartheid in the United States." Lecture presented at the Pacific Sociological Association Annual Conference, March 25, San Diego, CA.

Blalock, Hubert M. 1967. *Toward a Theory of Minority-Group Relations.* New York: Wiley.

Blankstein, Andrew, and Arin Gencer. 2006. "Gangs Cling to Westside Haunts." *Los Angeles Times,* July 19, B1.

Boga, Terence R. 1993. "Turf Wars: Street Gangs, Local Government, and the Battle for Public Space." *Harvard Civil Rights–Civil Liberties Law Review* 29:447–503.

Bonilla-Silva, Eduardo. 2001. *White Supremacy and Racism in the Post–Civil Rights Era.* Boulder, CO: Lynne Rienner Publishers.

Bowker, Geoffrey, and Susan Star. 1999. *Sorting Things Out: Classification and Its Consequences.* Cambridge, MA: MIT Press.

Bratton, William J., and Sean W. Malinowski. 2008. "Police Performance Management in Practice: Taking COMPSTAT to the Next Level." *Policing* 2 (3): 259–265.

"Building Setback Line." 1963. Council File no. 114090, City Planning Case nos. 11497 and 14744. Los Angeles: Los Angeles City Archives.

Cavafy, C. P. 1972. "Waiting for the Barbarians." 1904. In *C. P. Cavafy: Collected Poems.* Translated by Edmund Keeley and Philip Sherrard. Princeton, NJ: Princeton University Press, 1972.

Caldwell, Beth. 2010. "Criminalizing Day-to-Day Life: A Socio-legal Critique of Gang Injunctions." *American Journal of Criminal Law* 37 (3): 241–290.

Charles, Brian. 2013. "Lawsuit Aims to Curb L.A.'s Use of Gang Injunction Curfews." *Daily Breeze,* September 14. http://www.dailybreeze.com/general-news/20130914/lawsuit-aims-to-curb-las-use-of-gang-injunction-curfews.

Chesluk, Benjamin. 2004. "'Visible Signs of a City Out of Control': Community Policing in New York City." *Cultural Anthropology* 19 (2): 250–275.

La Cienega Heights Community Group. 2008. "Letter to Neighborhood Prosecutor." July. Los Angeles: La Cienega Heights Community Group.

City of Los Angeles Department of Building and Safety. 1960. "Application to Construct New Building and for Certificate of Occupancy, 8751 Guthrie Avenue." August 23. Los Angeles: Los Angeles Department of Building and Safety Records.

———. 1961a. "Application to Construct New Building and for Certificate of Occupancy, 1936 S. Corning Street." January 18. Los Angeles: Los Angeles Department of Building and Safety Records.

———. 1961b. "Application to Construct New Building and for Certificate of Occupancy, 2035 Chariton Street." August 3. Los Angeles: Los Angeles Department of Building and Safety Records.

———. 1962. "Application to Construct New Building and for Certificate of Occupancy, 2010 Chariton Street." August 8. Los Angeles: Los Angeles Department of Building and Safety Records.

City of Los Angeles Department of City Planning. 1966. "Recommendation of Commission Hearing Examiner." City Planning Case no. 19484. Los Angeles: Los Angeles City Archives.

———. 1969. "Recommendation of Commission Hearing Examiner." Council File no. 142400, City Planning Case nos. 22033 and 22032. Los Angeles: Los Angeles City Archives.

Coetzee, J. M. 1980. *Waiting for the Barbarians.* London: Penguin.

Collins, William J. 2006. "The Political Economy of State Fair Housing Laws before 1968." *Social Science History* 30 (1): 15–49.

Crawford, Adam. 1997. *The Local Governance of Crime: Appeals to Community and Partnerships.* Oxford: Clarendon Press.

Curtis, Mary. 1984. "Failure to Allay Fears of Hamihi Frustrates Advocates." *Los Angeles Times,* May 20, WS1.

Dauber, Mara. 2014. "Taking Liberties: The Los Angeles Police Department and the Civil Gang Injunction." Undergraduate honor thesis, Occidental College.

Davis, Mike. 2002. *Dead Cities.* New York: New Press.

———. 2006. *City of Quartz: Excavating the Future in Los Angeles.* New York: Verso.

DeMichele, Matthew T., and Peter B. Kraska. 2001. "Community Policing in Battle Garb: A Paradox or Coherent Strategy?" In *Militarizing the American Criminal Justice System: The Changing Roles of the Armed Forces and the Police,* edited by Peter B. Kraska. Boston: Northeastern University Press.

DiMaggio, Paul, and Walter Powell. 1983. "The Iron Cage Revisited: Institutional Isomorphism and Collective Rationality in Organizational Fields." *American Sociological Review* 48 (2): 147–160.

Duggan, Lisa. 2003. *The Twilight of Equality?* Boston: Beacon Press.

Duneier, Mitchell. 2001. *Sidewalk*. New York: Farrar, Straus & Giroux.

Eley, Lynn W., and Thomas W. Casstevens. 1968. *The Politics of Fair-Housing Legislation: State and Local Case Studies*. San Francisco: Chandler Publishing Co.

Elliott, Helen. 1999. "Staples Center Vision Is Fast Taking Shape." *Los Angeles Times*, February 23, D1.

Ellison, Treva, and Colby Lenz. 2012. "Gang Injunctions in Los Angeles: Mapping Police Violence." Lecture presented at ASE Commons, Department of American Studies and Ethnicity, University of Southern California, February 16, Los Angeles.

Faris, Gerald. 1970. "School Talking Out Its Problems." *Los Angeles Times*, January 29, WS1.

Feldman, Paul. 1987a. "Court Rejects City Attorney's Bid to Curb Westside Gang's Movements." *Los Angeles Times*, November 6, Metro section, 1.

———. 1987b. "Judge Raps City Atty.'s Bid to Neutralize Gangs." *Los Angeles Times*, December 11, Metro section, 3.

———. 1987c. "Drug Peddling Street Gang Holds Neighborhood in Fear." *Los Angeles Times*, November 16, Metro section, 1.

Ferrell, Jeff. 1995. "Urban Graffiti: Crime, Control, and Resistance." *Youth Society* 27 (1): 73–92.

Figlio, David N., and Maurice E. Lucas. 2004. "What's in a Grade? School Report Cards and the Housing Market." *American Economic Review* 94 (3): 591–604.

Fishman, Robert. 1987. *Bourgeois Utopias: The Rise and Fall of Suburbia*. New York: Basic Books.

Gains, Francesca, Peter C. John, and Gerry Stoker. 2005. "Path Dependency and the Reform of English Local Government." *Public Administration* 83 (1): 25–45.

Garland, David. 2001. *The Culture of Control: Crime and Order in Contemporary Society*. Chicago: University of Chicago Press.

Glassner, Barry. 1999. *The Culture of Fear*. New York: Basic Books.

Gordon, Colin. 2008. *Mapping Decline: St. Louis and the Fate of the American City*. Philadelphia: University of Pennsylvania Press.

GOV.UK. 2013. "Injunctions to Prevent Gang-Related Violence." March 26. https://www.gov.uk/injunctions-to-prevent-gang-related-violence.

Green, Donald P., Dara Z. Strolovitch, and Janelle S. Wong. 1998. "Defended Neighborhoods, Integration, and Racially Motivated Crime." *American Journal of Sociology* 104 (2): 372–403.

Greenberg, Cheryl Lynn. 2006. *Troubling the Waters: Black-Jewish Relations in the American Century*. Princeton, NJ: Princeton University Press.

Greenwood, Noel. 1972. "Transfers at Three L.A. Schools Banned: Board Acts to Maintain White, Minority Balance." *Los Angeles Times*, January 25, A1.

Grogger, Jeffrey. 2002. "The Effects of the Los Angeles County Gang Injunctions on Reported Crime." *Journal of Law and Economics* 45:69–90.

Harcourt, Bernard. 2001. *Illusion of Order: The False Promise of Broken Windows Policing*. Cambridge, MA: Harvard University Press.

Harton, Muriel. 1963. "Letter to Los Angeles City Clerk Walter C. Patterson." August 5. Council File no. 114090, City Planning Case nos. 11497 and 14744. Los Angeles: Los Angeles City Archives.

Haurin, Donald R., and David Brasington. 1996. "School Quality and Real House Prices: Inter- and Intrametropolitan Effects." *Journal of Housing Economics* 5 (4): 351–368.

Hayward, Keith J. 2004. *City Limits: Crime, Consumer Culture and the Urban Experience*. Portland, OR: Cavendish Publishing.

Hennigan, Karen M., and David Sloane. 2013. "Improving Civil Gang Injunctions." *Criminology and Public Policy* 12 (1): 7–41.

Herbert, Steve. 1997. *Policing Space: Territoriality and the Los Angeles Police Department.* Minneapolis: University of Minnesota Press.

———. 2001. "Policing the Contemporary City: Fixing Broken Windows or Shoring Up Neo-liberalism?" *Theoretical Criminology* 5 (4): 445–466.

Hinkle, Joshua C., and David Weisburd. 2008. "The Irony of Broken Windows Policing: A Micro-place Study of the Relationship between Disorder, Focused Police Crackdowns and Fear of Crime." *Journal of Criminal Justice* 36:503–512.

Jang, Hyunseok, Larry T. Hoover, and Brian A. Lawton. 2008. "Effect of Broken Windows Enforcement on Clearance Rates." *Journal of Criminal Justice* 36:529–538.

Johnston, Les. 1996. "What Is Vigilantism?" *British Journal of Criminology* 36 (2): 220–236.

Jones, Jack. 1970. "Jewish Group Pushes Integration Programs: Despite Black Nationalism, Anti-Semitism, AJC Says Negro Problem Must Be Solved." *Los Angeles Times,* August 11, B5.

Kane, Thomas J., Douglas O. Staiger, and Stephanie K. Riegg. 2005. "School Quality, Neighborhoods and Housing Prices: The Impacts of school Desegregation." *American Law and Economics Review* 8 (2): 183–212.

Kelley, Robin D. G. 1998. *Yo' Mama's Disfunktional! Fighting the Culture Wars in Urban America.* Boston: Beacon Press.

Klein, Malcolm. 1998. "The Problem of Street Gangs and Problem-Oriented Policing." In *Problem-Oriented Policing: Crime-Specific Problems, Critical Issues, and Making POP Work,* edited by Tara O'Connor and Shelley Anne Grant, 57–86. Washington, DC: Police Executive Research Forum.

Kundera, Milan. 1999. *The Unbearable Lightness of Being.* New York: Harper Perennial Modern Classics.

Leonard, David Jason. 2003. "'No Jews and No Coloreds Are Welcome in This Town': Constructing Coalitions in Post/War Los Angeles." *Dissertation Abstracts International A: The Humanities and Social Sciences* 64 (2).

Levenson, Norman, and Rae Levenson. 1963. "Letter to Los Angeles City Clerk Walter C. Patterson." August 6. Council File no. 114090, City Planning Case nos. 11497 and 14744. Los Angeles: Los Angeles City Archives.

Levin-Waldman, Oren M. 2009. "Urban Path Dependency Theory and the Living Wage." *Journal of Socio-economics* 38 (4): 672–683.

Livingston, Debra. 1997. "Police Discretion and the Quality of Life in Public Places: Courts, Communities, and the New Policing." *Columbia Law Review* 97:551–672.

Lockard, Duane. 1968. *Toward Equal Opportunity: A Study of State and Local Antidiscrimination Laws.* New York: Macmillan.

Los Angeles County District Attorney's Office. 2011. "Civil Action Targets Rival San Gabriel Valley Gangs." April 19. Los Angeles: Los Angeles County District Attorney's Office.

Los Angeles Department of City Planning. 2001. "Housing Element: City of Los Angeles General Plan." Los Angeles: Los Angeles Department of City Planning.

Los Angeles Police Department. 1980–2011. *Statistical Digest.* Los Angeles: Los Angeles Police Department.

Los Angeles Times. 1963. "School Board Speakers on Bias Booed, Cheered." September 20, A2.

———. 1973a. "Boredom and Tension Replace 'Golden Age.'" June 10, 1.

———. 1973b. "Bureaucracy Creates Frustration at School." June 14, 3.

———. 1973c. "Frustration Fills Hamilton High Academic Life." June 11, A1.

———. 1973d. "Hamilton High Seeks Answers in Black, White." June 12, A1.

———. 1973e. "Security: Hamilton High Seeks Security Behind Fences." June 13, A1.

———. 1993. "The Issue: Using Abatement Laws to Stop Drug Trade: FOR: James K. Hahn." March 8.

Lyons, William. 1999. *The Politics of Community Policing: Rearranging the Power to Punish.* Ann Arbor: University of Michigan Press.

Mahoney, J. 2001. "Path-Dependent Explanations of Regime Change: Central America in Comparative Perspective." *Studies in Comparative International Development* 36 (1): 111–141.

Maxson, Cheryl L. 2004. "Civil Gang Injunctions: The Ambiguous Case of the National Migration of a Gang Enforcement Strategy." In *American Youth Gangs at the Millennium,* edited by Finn Esbensen, Larry Gaines, and Steve Tibbetts. Long Grove, IL: Waveland.

Maxson, Cheryl L., Karen Hennigan, and David Sloane. 2003. "For the Sake of the Neighborhood? Civil Gang Injunctions as a Gang Intervention Tool in Southern California." In *Policing Gangs and Youth Violence,* edited by Scott H. Decker, 239–266. Belmont, CA: Thomson/Wadsworth.

McCurdy, Jack. 1968. "New Boundaries for 14 Schools Proposed as Integration Move." *Los Angeles Times,* April 2, 3.

Meares, Tracey M., and Dan M. Kahan. 1998. "Laws and (Norms of) Order in the Inner City." *Law and Society Review* 32:805–822.

Mercy Housing. 2012. "Celebrating Wilmington's New Dana Strand." December 14. http://mercyhousingblog.org/2012/12/14/celebrating-transformation -wilmingtons-new-dana-strand.

Minear, Mrs. William. 1963. "Letter to Los Angeles City Clerk Walter C. Patterson." n.d. Council File no. 114090, City Planning Case nos. 11497 and 14744. Los Angeles: Los Angeles City Archives.

Miranda, Eduardo Mendoza. 2008. "Gang Injunctions and Community Participation." *Dissertation Abstracts International, A: The Humanities and Social Sciences* 68(10).

"Motion." 1970, April 9. Council File no. 142400, City Planning Case nos. 22033 and 22032. Los Angeles: Los Angeles City Archives.

Myers, Thomas A. 2009. "The Unconstitutionality, Ineffectiveness, and Alternatives of Gang Injunctions." *Michigan Journal of Race and Law* 14 (2): 285–306.

Nafisi, Azar. 2003. *Reading Lolita in Tehran: A Memoir in Books.* New York: Random House.

Nagin, Daniel S. 1999. "Criminal Deterrence Research at the Outset of the Twenty-First Century." *Crime and Justice* 23:1–37.

O'Deane, Matthew David. 2007. "Effectiveness of Gang Injunctions in California: A Multicounty 25-Year Study." *Dissertation Abstracts International, A: The Humanities and Social Sciences* 68 (9).

Office of Los Angeles City Councilman Zev Yaroslavsky. 1987. "Letter to Los Angeles City Attorney James K. Hahn." April 13. Los Angeles: Office of Los Angeles City Councilman Zev Yaroslavsky.

Office of the City Attorney of Los Angeles. 1987. "Notice to Abate Public Nuisance and of Intent to Seek A Preliminary and Permanent Injunction in Lieu of Voluntary Abatement." Los Angeles: Office of the City Attorney of Los Angeles.

———. 2012. "Gang Injunction Removal Petition Program Statistics." Criminal

Division, Gang Injunctions. Los Angeles: Office of the City Attorney of Los Angeles.

———. 2013. "Current Citywide Gang Injunction Map." Criminal Division, Gang Injunctions. Los Angeles: Office of the City Attorney of Los Angeles.

Oliver, Marilyn. 1989. "A Westside 'Pocket of Affordability.'" *Los Angeles Times*, December 10, Home edition, 2.

O'Sullivan, Arthur, Terri A. Sexton, and Steven M. Sheffrin. 1995. *Property Taxes and Tax Revolts.* New York: Cambridge University Press.

Parenti, Christian. 2001. *Lockdown America: Police and Prisons in the Age of Crisis.* New York: New Left Books.

Poston, Ben and Joel Rubin. 2014. "LAPD Misclassified Nearly 1,200 Violent Crimes as Minor Offenses." *Los Angeles Times*, August 9. http://www.latimes.com/local/la-me-crimestats-lapd-20140810-story.html#page=1.

Quillian, Lincoln, and Devah Pager. 2001. "Black Neighbors, Higher Crime? The Role of Racial Stereotypes in Evaluations of Neighborhood Crime." *American Journal of Sociology* 107 (3): 717–767.

Roberts, Dorothy E. 1999. "Race, Vagueness, and the Social Meaning of Order Maintenance Policing." *Journal of Criminal Law and Criminology* 89 (3): 775–836.

Roberts, John E., and Roy T. Davis. 1963. "Letter to Los Angeles City Council." June 25. Council File no. 114090, City Planning Case nos. 11497 and 14744. Los Angeles: Los Angeles City Archives.

Romero, Dennis. 2013. "Can Echo Park Hipsters Be Safe from Gangs?" *LA Weekly*, June 18. http://www.laweekly.com/informer/2013/06/18/can-echo-park-hipsters-be-safe-from-gangs.

Sampson, Robert J., and Stephen W. Raudenbush. 2004. "Seeing Disorder: Neighborhood Stigma and the Social Construction of 'Broken Windows.'" *Social Psychology Quarterly* 67 (4): 319–342.

Santa Cruz, Nicole. 2014. "The Homicide Report: Family Pleads for Witnesses to Come Forward in Rush Hour Shooting Death." *Los Angeles Times*, May 25.

Santos, Xuan, and Rebecca Romo. 2007. "Gang Injunction Laws." In *Battleground: Criminal Justice,* edited by Gregg Barak, 1:303–310. Westport, CT: Greenwood Press.

Sasson, Theodore. 1995. *Crime Talk: How Citizens Construct a Problem.* New York: Aldine de Gruyter.

Sears, David O., and Jack Citrin. 1982. *Tax Revolt: Something for Nothing in California.* Cambridge, MA: Harvard University Press.

Sennett, Richard. 1980. *Authority.* New York: Vintage Books.

Shuit, Douglas P. 2001. "MTA OKs Downtown-Westside Light Rail." *Los Angeles Times,* June 29, B4.

Siegel, Loren. 2003. "Gangs and the Law." In *Gangs and Society: Alternative Perspectives,* edited by Louis Kontos, David Brotherton, and Luis Barrios, 213–227. New York: Columbia University Press.

Simmers, T. J., and David Wharton. 1999. "How the Game Was Played." In "Taking Center Stage (The Staples Center)," special issue. *Los Angeles Times Magazine,* October 10. http://articles.latimes.com/1999/oct/10/magazine/tm-20650.

Simon, Jonathan. 2007. *Governing through Crime.* New York: Oxford University Press.

Smith, Doug. 1972. "School on Spot as Integrated Educational Unit." *Los Angeles Times,* May 7, WS1.

Staples, William. 2000. *Everyday Surveillance: Vigilance and Visibility in Postmodern Life.* Lanham, MD: Rowman & Littlefield.

Stevenson, Rulon W., and Nellie A. Stevenson. 1963. "Letter to Los Angeles City

Clerk Walter C. Patterson." n.d. Council File no. 114090, City Planning Case nos. 11497 and 14744. Los Angeles: Los Angeles City Archives.

Stewart, Eric A., Erik P. Baumer, Rod K. Brunson, and Ronald D. Simons. 2009. "Neighborhood Racial Context and Perceptions of Police-Based Racial Discrimination among Black Youth." *Criminology* 47 (3): 847–887.

Stewart, Gary. 1998. "Black Codes and Broken Windows: The Legacy of Racial Hegemony in Anti-gang Civil Injunctions." *Yale Law Journal* 107 (7): 2249–2279.

Stuntz, William J. 2011. *The Collapse of American Criminal Justice.* Cambridge, MA: Harvard University Press.

Terrill, William, and Michael D. Reisig. 2003. "Neighborhood Context and Police Use of Force." *Journal of Research in Crime and Delinquency* 40 (3): 291–321.

Tlacil, Ethel. 1963. "Letter to Los Angeles City Clerk Walter C. Patterson." n.d. Council File no. 114090, City Planning Case nos. 11497 and 14744. Los Angeles: Los Angeles City Archives.

Tolnay, Stewart E., E. M. Beck, and James L. Massey. 1989. "Black Lynchings: The Power Threat Hypothesis Revisited." *Social Forces* 67:605–623.

Trojanowicz, Robert, and Bonnie Bucqueroux. 1990. *Community Policing: A Contemporary Perspective.* Cincinnati: Anderson Publishing Co.

Trombley, William. 1979. "Doubt Cast on Usefulness of Magnet Schools." *Los Angeles Times*, December 17, C1.

———. 1980. "Policies Lead to Busing Avoidance, Report Says." *Los Angeles Times*, June 2, C1.

Turpin, Dick. 1967a. "School Board OKs 10 Special Centers to Boost Integration." *Los Angles Times*, January 4, F7.

———. 1967b. "Major Integration Plan to Be Tried This Year." *Los Angles Times*, January 11, A6.

Urban Land Institute. 2009. "An Advisory Services Panel Report: Jordan Downs, Los Angeles, California." Washington, DC: Urban Land Institute.

U.S. Bureau of the Census. 1960a. "Race: Census Tract 29690000, Los Angeles County, California." Washington, DC: U.S. Bureau of the Census. Accessed through *Social Explorer,* http://www.socialexplorer.com.

———. 1960b. "Occupation: Census Tract 29690000, Los Angeles County, California." Washington, DC: U.S. Bureau of the Census. Accessed through *Social Explorer,* http://www.socialexplorer.com.

———. 1960c. "Foreign Born: Census Tract 29690000, Los Angeles County, California." Washington, DC: U.S. Bureau of the Census. Accessed through *Social Explorer,* http://www.socialexplorer.com.

———. 1960d. "Country of Origin: Census Tract 29690000, Los Angeles County, California." Washington, DC: U.S. Bureau of the Census. Accessed through *Social Explorer,* http://www.socialexplorer.com.

———. 1970. "Race: Census Tract 2696, Los Angeles County, California." Washington, DC: U.S. Bureau of the Census. Accessed through *Social Explorer,* http://www.socialexplorer.com.

———. 1980a. "Race by Spanish Origin Status: Census Tract 2696, Los Angeles County, California." Washington, DC: U.S. Bureau of the Census. Accessed through *Social Explorer,* http://www.socialexplorer.com.

———. 1980b. "Race: Census Tract 2166, Los Angeles County, California." Washington, DC: U.S. Bureau of the Census. Accessed through *Social Explorer,* http://www.socialexplorer.com.

———. 1980c. "Race: Census Tract 2695, Los Angeles County, California." Washington, DC: U.S. Bureau of the Census. Accessed through *Social Explorer,* http://www.socialexplorer.com.

———. 1980d. "Average Household Income (in 1979 Dollars): Census Tract 2696, Los Angeles County, California." Washington, DC: U.S. Bureau of the Census. Accessed through *Social Explorer,* http://www.socialexplorer.com.

———. 1980e. "Average Household Income (in 1979 Dollars): Census Tract 2695, Los Angeles County, California." Washington, DC: U.S. Bureau of the Census. Accessed through *Social Explorer,* http://www.socialexplorer.com.

———. 1980f. "Tenure: Census Tract 2695, Los Angeles County, California." Washington, DC: U.S. Bureau of the Census. Accessed through *Social Explorer,* http://www.socialexplorer.com.

———. 1990a. "Race: Census Tract 2696, Los Angeles County, California." Washington, DC: U.S. Bureau of the Census. Accessed through *Social Explorer,* http://www.socialexplorer.com.

———. 1990b. "Hispanic Origin by Race: Census Tract 2696, Los Angeles County, California." Washington, DC: U.S. Bureau of the Census. Accessed through *Social Explorer,* http://www.socialexplorer.com.

———. 1990c. "1990 Census of Population and Housing, Public Law 94-171 Data (official), Age by Race and Hispanic Origin, Los Angeles County California." Washington, DC: U.S. Bureau of the Census.

———. 2000a. "Race Alone or in Combination and Hispanic or Latino: 2000, Census 2000 Summary File 1 (SF 1) 100-Percent Data." Washington, DC: U.S. Bureau of the Census. Accessed through *American Fact Finder,* http://factfinder2.census.gov.

———. 2000b. "Profile of Selected Economic Characteristics: 2000, Census 2000 Summary File 4 (SF 4)—Sample Data." Washington, DC: U.S. Bureau of the Census. Accessed through *American Fact Finder,* http://factfinder2.census.gov.

———. 2000c. "Profile of General Demographic Characteristics: 2000, Census 2000 Summary File 2 (SF 2) 100-Percent Data." Washington, DC: U.S. Bureau of the Census. Accessed through *American Fact Finder,* http://factfinder2.census.gov.

———. 2000d. "Profile of Selected Economic Characteristics: 2000, Census 2000 Summary File 4 (SF 4)—Sample Data." Washington, DC: U.S. Bureau of the Census. Accessed through *American Fact Finder,* http://factfinder2.census.gov.

———. 2000e. "Profile of General Demographic Characteristics: 2000, Census 2000 Summary File 2 (SF 2) 100-Percent Data." Washington, DC: U.S. Bureau of the Census. Accessed through *American Fact Finder,* http://factfinder2.census.gov.

———. 2000f. "Race and Hispanic or Latino: 2000, Census 2000 Summary File 1 (SF 1) 100-Percent Data." Washington, DC: U.S. Bureau of the Census. Accessed through *American Fact Finder,* http://factfinder2.census.gov.

———. 2007–2011. "ACS Demographic and Housing Estimates, 2007–2011: American Community Survey 5 Year Estimates, Los Angeles County, California." Washington, DC: U.S. Bureau of the Census.

———. 2010a. "Profile of General Population and Housing Characteristics: Census Tract 2696.01, Los Angeles County, California." Washington, DC: U.S. Bureau of the Census. Accessed through *American Fact Finder,* http://factfinder2.census.gov.

———. 2010b. "Profile of General Population and Housing Characteristics: Census Tract 2696.02, Los Angeles County, California." Washington, DC: U.S. Bureau of the Census. Accessed through *American Fact Finder,* http://factfinder2.census.gov.

———. 2010c. "Profile of General Population and Housing Characteristics: Census Tract 2170.02, Los Angeles County, California." Washington, DC: U.S. Bureau of the Census. Accessed through *American Fact Finder,* http://factfinder2.census.gov.

———. 2010d. "Profile of General Population and Housing Characteristics: Census Tract 2695, Los Angeles County, California." Washington, DC: U.S. Bureau of the Census. Accessed through *American Fact Finder,* http://factfinder2.census.gov.

Vannoy, Brittany. 2009. "Turning Their Lives Around: California Cities Pioneer Injunction Removal Procedures." *Journal of the National Association of Administrative Law Judiciary* 29 (1): 283–324.

Vigil, James Diego. 2003. "Urban Violence and Street Gangs." *Annual Review of Anthropology* 32:225–242.

Williams, Sabrina L. 2003. "From HOPE VI to HOPE Sick?" *Dollars and Sense,* July/August. http://www.dollarsandsense.org/archives/2003/0703williams.html.

Wilson, James Q., and George L. Kelling. 1982. "Broken Windows." *Atlantic Monthly,* March. http://www.theatlantic.com/magazine/archive/1982/03/broken -windows/304465.

Xu, Yili, Mora L. Fiedler, and Karl H. Flaming. 2005. "Discovering the Impact of Community Policing: The Broken Windows Thesis, Collective Efficacy, and Citizens' Judgment." *Journal of Research in Crime and Delinquency* 42(2):147–186.

———. 2014. "People of the State of California; Plaintiff; vs. Mike Feuer, Los Angeles City Attorney; Anne Tremblay, Assistant Los Angeles City Attorney, Director of Gang Unit; Jim McDougal, Assistant Los Angeles City Attorney." Los Angeles: Youth Justice Coalition.

Zuckerman, Marvin, and Lea Bleviss. 1973. "Hamilton High: A Vivid Symbol." *Los Angeles Times,* July 13, A7.

Cases Cited *City of Los Angeles v. Playboy Gangster Crips.* 1987a. Sample Law Enforcement Declarations. Los Angeles Police Department Officer, October 26.

———. 1987b. Sample Law Enforcement Declarations. Los Angeles Police Department Officer, October 24.

———. 1987c. Sample Law Enforcement Declarations. Los Angeles County Probation Officer, September 3.

———. 1987d. Sample Law Enforcement Declarations. Los Angeles Police Department Officer, October 27.

———. 1987e. Declaration of Deputy City Attorney, October 30.

———. 1987f. Sample Law Enforcement Declarations. Los Angeles Police Department Officer, October 26.

People ex rel. Gallo v. Acuna. 1997. No. S046980 (14 Cal. 4th 1090).

People v. Blythe St. Gang. 1993. No. LC 020525, slip op. at 1 (Cal. Super. Ct. Los Angeles County, April 7). Declaration by Los Angeles Police Department Officer, February 8.

People v. Playboy Gangster Crips. 1987. No. WEC 118860 (Cal. Super. Ct. Los Angeles County, December 11).

People v. Big Top Locos. 2013. No. BC511444 (Cal. Super. Ct. Los Angeles County, September 24).

———. 2013a. Declaration of Los Angeles Police Department Officer, May 18.

———. 2013b. Declaration of Los Angeles Police Department Officer, June 6.

———. 2013c. Declaration of Los Angeles Police Department Officer, June 5.

———. 2013d. Declaration of Los Angeles Police Department Officer, June 4.

Vasquez v. Rackauckas. 2013. 734 F. 3d 1025 (Court of Appeals, 9th Circuit, November 5).

Index

ABOUT THE AUTHOR

ANA MUÑIZ is director of the Dream Resource Center at the UCLA Labor Center, an institute for research, education, and policy on undocumented youth immigrant issues in Los Angeles, California.

Anthony M. Platt, *The Child Savers: The Invention of Delinquency*, 40th Anniversary Edition with an introduction and critical commentaries compiled by Miroslava Chávez-García

Jeffrey Ian Ross, ed., *The Globalization of Supermax Prisons*

Dawn L. Rothe and Christopher W. Mullins, eds., *State Crime: Current Perspectives*

Jodi Schorb, *Reading Prisoners: Literature, Literacy, and the Transformation of American Punishment, 1700–1845*

Susan F. Sharp, *Hidden Victims: The Effects of the Death Penalty on Families of the Accused*

Susan F. Sharp and Juanita Ortiz, *Mean Lives and Mean Laws: Oklahoma's Women Prisoners*

Robert H. Tillman and Michael L. Indergaard, *Pump and Dump: The Rancid Rules of the New Economy*

Mariana Valverde, *Law and Order: Images, Meanings, Myths*

Michael Welch, *Crimes of Power & States of Impunity: The U.S. Response to Terror*

Michael Welch, *Scapegoats of September 11th: Hate Crimes and State Crimes in the War on Terror*

Saundra D. Westervelt and Kimberly J. Cook, *Life after Death Row: Exonerees' Search for Community and Identity*

ation can be obtained
ting.com
A
0915

9 780813 569758